Global Shakespeares

The Global Shakespeares series, edited by Alexa Alice Joubin, explores the global afterlife of Shakespearean drama, poetry and motifs in their literary, performative and digital forms of expression in the twentieth and twenty-first centuries. Disseminating big ideas and cutting-edge research in e-book and print formats, this series captures global Shakespeares as they evolve.

Amrita Sen
Editor

Digital Shakespeares from the Global South

palgrave
macmillan

Editor
Amrita Sen
University of Calcutta
Kolkata, India

ISSN 2947-8901   ISSN 2947-891X   (electronic)
Global Shakespeares
ISBN 978-3-031-04786-2   ISBN 978-3-031-04787-9   (eBook)
https://doi.org/10.1007/978-3-031-04787-9

Cover illustration: © John Rawsterne/patternhead.com

This Palgrave Macmillan imprint is published by the registered company Springer Nature
Switzerland AG
The registered company address is: Gewerbestrasse 11, 6330 Cham, Switzerland

In Memory of my father, Gautam Sen, who enjoyed Shakespeare and introduced me to the digital.

ACKNOWLEDGEMENTS

This book has incurred many debts along its way. I am especially grateful to Alexa Alice Joubin for all her support and generosity. This volume would not be possible without her. Thanks also to Eileen Srebernik and the editorial team at Palgrave Macmillan. This book came into being during the pandemic, at a time of personal loss. The friendships of Jyotsna G. Singh, Chinhita Bose, Amrita Dhar, and Jennifer Wood have meant a lot to me.

Souvik Mukherjee is still the person who comes to the rescue for all things, big and small. I especially appreciate our conversations on the digital that helped shape the journey of this book. A special thanks to Mira Bella Mukherjee who has taught me to look at Shakespeare performances with new eyes.

CONTENTS

NOTES ON CONTRIBUTORS

Craig Heidi is Assistant Professor of English at Texas A&M University, editor of the *World Shakespeare Bibliography*, and co-editor of *Early Modern Dramatic Paratexts*. She researches dramatic production during the theatrical prohibition of 1642 to 1660, the significance of rags and rag collectors in early European textual culture, and dramatic paratexts. She has published articles and book chapters in *English Literary Renaissance, Huntington Library Quarterly*, and various edited collections. Her first monograph, *Theatre Closure and the Paradoxical Rise of English Renaissance Drama*, is under contract with Cambridge University Press.

Estill Laura is a Canada Research Chair in Digital Humanities and Associate Professor of English at St. Francis Xavier University (Nova Scotia, Canada). She is a former editor of the *World Shakespeare Bibliography*, author of *Dramatic Extracts in Seventeenth-Century English Manuscripts*, and co-editor of *Early Modern Studies after the Digital Turn* and *Early British Drama in Manuscript*. Her most recent articles and chapters have appeared in *The Seventeenth Century, Humanities, Doing More Digital Humanities, Shakespeare's Theatrical Documents*, and *The Arden Research Handbook of Shakespeare and Textual Studies*.

Joubin Alexa Alice is Professor of English, Women's, Gender and Sexuality Studies, Theatre, International Affairs, and East Asian Languages and Literatures at George Washington University in Washington, D.C., where she serves as founding Co-director of the Digital Humanities Institute.

Her latest book is *Shakespeare and East Asia* (Oxford University Press, 2021), which brings film and theatre studies together to bear on deep structural connections among Asian and Anglophone performances.

Mukherjee Souvik is Assistant Professor in Cultural Studies at the Centre for Studies in Social Sciences, Calcutta. He is the author of two monographs, *Videogames and Storytelling: Reading Games and Playing Books* (Palgrave Macmillan 2015) and *Videogames and Postcolonialism: Empire Plays Back* (Springer UK 2017), as well as many articles and book chapters in national and international publications. His databases on the Dutch Cemetery at Chinsurah, the Scottish Cemetery in Kolkata and the nineteenth-century Bengali industrialist, Mutty Lall Seal are all available open-access. He has been a board-member of the Digital Games Research Association (DiGRA) and a founder-member of DHARTI, the Digital Humanities group in India. He has been named a "DiGRA Distinguished Scholar" in 2019.

Sen Amrita is Associate Professor and Deputy Director, UGC-HRDC, University of Calcutta, and affiliated member of the Department of English. She is co-editor of *Civic Performance: Pageantry and Entertainments in Early Modern London* (Routledge 2020), and a special issue of the *Journal for Early Modern Cultural Studies* on "Alternative Histories of the East India Company" (2017). She has published essays and book chapters on East India Company women, Bollywood Shakespeares, and early modern ethnography.

Thurman Chris is Professor of English and Director of the Tsikinya-Chaka Centre at the University of the Witwatersrand (Johannesburg, South Africa). He is the editor of *South African Essays on 'Universal' Shakespeare* (2014), *Sport versus Art: A South African Contest* (2010) and thirteen volumes of *Shakespeare in Southern Africa*. His other books are the monograph *Guy Butler: Reassessing a South African Literary Life* (2010); *Text Bites*, an anthology for high schools (2009); and two collections of arts journalism, *At Large: Reviewing the Arts in South Africa* (2012) and *Still at Large: Dispatches from South Africa's Frontiers of Politics and Art* (2017). He is president of the Shakespeare Society of Southern Africa and founder of Shakespeare ZA (shakespeare.org.za).

LIST OF FIGURES

CHAPTER 1

Introduction: Experiencing Digital Shakespeares in the Global South

Amrita Sen

Abstract This introductory chapter interrogates what the Global South signifies as a geo-political and economic space, and how that effects the way we understand Shakespeare adaptations in the digital age. Teaching, learning, and adaptations of Shakespeare have a long history in the Global South, usually mediated through colonial experiences. In recent years with the expansion of the digital marketplace in the Global South, Shakespeare has also made the digital leap. At the same time, not everyone has equal access to digital tools, disparities that have become even more urgent during the Covid-19 pandemic. To speak of digital Shakespeares in the Global South is to address questions of digital divide. Insufficient bandwidth and access to digital equipment, all factor into how digital Shakespeares are experienced in classrooms and homes.

Keywords Digital Shakespeares · Global South · Digital Divide

A. Sen (✉)
University of Calcutta, Kolkata, West Bengal, India
e-mail: dr.amritasen.earlymodern@gmail.com

A. Sen (ed.), *Digital Shakespeares from the Global South*,
Global Shakespeares, https://doi.org/10.1007/978-3-031-04787-9_1

1

In January 2017, as part of "Shakespeare Lives" or the worldwide events to mark William Shakespeare's 400th death anniversary, the British Council in India adopted a multi-faceted approach to attract visitors to its stall at the International Kolkata Book Fair (IKBF) which is one of Asia's largest book exhibition-cum-fairs.[1] Alongside the traditional display of books and the screening of short films based on Shakespeare's plays, visitors were encouraged to engage with the digital avatar of the Shakespearean text through "Mix the Play." An "interactive video platform," the British Council's "Mix the Play" at the IKBF invited users to play with and (re)create their own versions of *Romeo and Juliet* based on scenes crafted by Roysten Abel, the noted Indian theater director and founder of the Indian Shakespeare Company.[2] The users or players of the interactive web application could choose their own stage settings, actors, music, and cultural interpretations. Similar to a game-play environment, the users could thus come up with multiple re-enactments of the iconic balcony scene, thereby (re)playing Shakespeare again and again. This gamification of Shakespeare's play, however, was located within an Indian context—not only because of the venue of the IKBF or for its use of Indian actors and director, but also because the themes themselves addressed specific Indian concerns. For instance, the choice of scenes included a sari-clad Hindu Juliet locked away from her Muslim Romeo, or the booming Indian corporate world throwing a wedge between two star-crossed urban lovers. Unlike "Mix the Play's" *A Midsummer Night's Dream* which was made earlier in collaboration with The Old Vic Theatre, *Romeo and Juliet* was thus imagined and advertised as the *Indian* digital adaptation of the bard. The heterogeneous mix of IKBF visitors hailing from different socio-economic backgrounds, linguistic as well as technological proficiencies, could thus not only interact with the physical Shakespearean texts that were readily available in many of the fair stalls, but could also experience, perhaps for some for the first time, digital Shakespeares.

---

[1] Ghosh, "Kolkata book fair put off due to COVID-19." Started in 1976, the IKBF is an annual ten-day non-trade fair that attracts around 2 million visitors. Alongside major global and regional publishers, the fair also sees large participation from independent book publishers and sellers. Books sold or exhibited are from multiple languages, including some from endangered Indian language groups.

[2] British Council, "Mix the Play: *Romeo and Juliet*".

The British Council's decision to play along with the Indianized *Romeo and Juliet* at the IKBF raises questions familiar to Global Shakespeares—localizing the bard, debates over language, the relation between production houses in London or Stratford and those in the post-colonies. At the same time "Mix the Play" raises other, newer, questions—those of digital literacy and accessibility, the relation between digital participation and socio-economic privilege, the complex role of transmedia Shakespeare adaptations, and political agency in the Global South. This then is a brave new Global Shakespeare. Shakespeare's transition to the digital age, his ever expanding presence on YouTube, social media, gaming or Over the Top (OTT) platforms, and Digital Humanities (DH) projects opens up new possibilities as well as challenges on how we continue to interpret the bard. Commenting on the ubiquity of digital media in our modern lives, Valerie M. Fazel and Louise Geddes coin the term "Shakespeare User" to describe those operating within a widening "software culture" with its complex relation with agency and consumerism.[3] Networked Shakespeare comes with the lure of unprecedented levels of access—particularly to those outside of academia or elite performance institutions—and the possibility of reaching underrepresented communities.[4]

Recent scholarship has been quick to highlight many of the cultural, aesthetic, and political stakes of Shakespeare in cyberspace.[5] What is often missing from these conversations, however, is how digital Shakespeares are created or experienced outside of Anglo-America, in spaces that often coincide with the post-colonies marked by unequal access to digital resources and complex histories of Shakespeare transmissions.

[3] Fazel and Geddes, "Introduction: The Shakespeare User," 4.

[4] See Fazel and Geddes, 3–7; Carson and Kirwan, "Shakespeare and the Digital World Introduction," 5.

[5] See for instance the special issue on *Shakespeare and New Media* (*Shakespeare Quarterly* 2010), Christy Carson and Peter Kirwan's *Shakespeare and the Digital World* (2014), Stephen O'Neill's *Shakespeare and YouTube: New Media Forms of the Bard* (2014) and *Broadcast Your Shakespeare: Continuity and Change Across Media* (2017), Valerie M. Fazel and Louise Geddes' *The Shakespeare User: Critical and Creative Appropriations in a Networked Culture* (2017), Janelle Jenstad, Mark Kaethler, and Jennifer Roberts-Smith's *Shakespeare's Language in Digital Media: Old Words, New Tools* (2018), Maurizio Calbi and Stephen O'Neill's special issue *Shakespeare and Social Media* (*Borrowers and Lenders* 2016) and most recently Diana Henderson and Kyle Sebastian Vitale's *Shakespeare and Digital Pedagogy: Case Studies and Strategies* (2021).

From the other side of the spectrum, while scholarship on Global Shakespeares has helped bring to the forefront the rich diversity of Shakespeare adaptations in text, stage, and on-screen, its ambit has only recently been increasing to include the digital.[6] I offer a truism here: Shakespeare has entered the digital age, but not everyone experiences the digital in the same way. But then, of course, not everyone experiences Shakespeare the same way. To talk of digital Shakespeares in the Global South is to talk of appropriation, not only of Shakespeare, but also of the digital. It is to adapt tools to the needs and bandwidth of communities, to come up with alternate uses for existing platforms, it is to negotiate language in new ways. The need to examine digital cultures in the Global South and the role of Shakespeare, have become all the more urgent in the wake of the Coronavirus pandemic that began in early 2020 (although the variant itself was detected in late 2019). As schools, universities, and theaters closed, switching almost exclusively and abruptly to the virtual space, new questions emerged on digital participation. As digital usage grows in the Global South, bringing a vast population under the ambit of new technologies, a re-evaluation of the role of Shakespeare and Shakespeare studies in these emergent cyberspaces becomes all the more important. This collection hopes to start new conversations on pedagogic practices, online archives, digital performances, and social media platforms that make visible the critical as well as creative adaptations of Shakespeare in the Global South.

Interrogating the Global South

The Global South as a term does not rest easy. To speak of the "Global South" is to also speak of and remember other shifting and overlapping terms such as post-colonial, decolonial, and Third World.[7] Made popular after the 2003 United Nations Development Program named "Forging a Global South," the term offers an alternative to the Post World War II and

[6] For scholarship on digital Shakespeares within a global context see Minami, "What's in a name? Shakespeare and Japanese pop culture;" Kullman, "Shakespeare on the Internet: Global and South Asian Appropriations"; Ick, "The Performance Archive and the Digital Construction of Asian Shakespeare".

[7] See for instance Mignolo, *The Darker Side of the Renaissance* where he links decolonialism to the Bandung Conference of 1955 (xii). The Conference was, in fact, also one of the key events that led to calls for greater South-South cooperation and the Non-Aligned Movement.

Cold War category of the Third World.[8] In this sense, the rise of the term is tied to the collapse of the Soviet Union, and an attempt to locate more agency to the economically weaker nations of Asia, Africa, and South America that were also erstwhile colonies and later mostly members of the Non-Aligned Movement.[9] The Global South is thus a promise, or at least an aspiration, for collective growth and cooperation amongst nations liberated from European colonization. It is also an acknowledgment of shared histories of marginalization and their accompanying challenges as well as a call for greater cultural exchanges.

As Sandra Young argues, however, the idea of "Southerliness" can be traced back to the early modern period, with European geographers and cartographers during this pivotal period of global contact, distinguishing between the "southern climes" or "Southern Nations" and the "Northern People."[10] Driving the point home, Young clarifies: "the distinction between 'South' and 'North' emerged during the early modern expansionist period as a key mechanism for establishing a racial hierarchy on a global scale."[11] The Global South carries with it this legacy of colonial history, and as a category at times appears obviously flawed. For instance, not all modern nations in the Southern Hemisphere (notably Australia and New Zealand) fall within the ambit of the Global South; on the other hand, the geographical North is also home to several countries or regions that remain economically underdeveloped and have their own complex histories of political disenfranchisement. Furthermore, the Global South is far from homogeneous. The disparity lies not just amongst but also within nations. As Arif Dirlik cautions, "these societies themselves are under pressure from neoliberal globalization [...] and suffer some of the consequences of uneven development that is a structural characteristic of global capitalism."[12] These, often acute, social, and economic disparities *within* the Global South also affect the levels of digital participation of citizens, which in a digitized age, can have disastrous consequences. For instance, the Indian government during its rollout of the vaccination program for Covid-19, made prior registration on its digital platforms such as CoWIN

---

[8] See Dirlik, "Introduction," 12–13; Young, *Shakespeare in the Global South*, 6–8.

[9] Levander and Mignolo, "Introduction," 3; Kloß 2.

[10] Young, 4–5.

[11] Young, 5.

[12] Dirlick, 17.

and Aarogya Setu compulsory for those between the ages of 18 and 45. This digital insistence resulted in unequal access to the vaccination program, wherein those without smartphones or computers as well as those not proficient in the English language were left out.[13] Following outcry from different quarters, including the Indian Supreme Court, unregistered walk-ins were eventually allowed in government centers, but the rules remained in place for all private vaccination sites.[14] Moreover, vaccination records continue to be primarily digitally accessible.

Despite its shortcomings, the Global South as an economic and cultural category continues to grow in popularity. Recent titles ranging from *Affordable Housing in the Urban Global South: Seeking Sustainable Solutions* (2014) to *Horror Fiction in the Global South* (2021) are indicative of the broad reach of Global South as a term. Part of its continuing relevance draws upon its promise of what is often understood as "South-South" cooperation. Some of the earliest usages of Global South emerged as part of a new vocabulary aimed at projecting greater agency and economic cooperation amongst marginalized nations in South America, Africa, and Asia. The Global South then, makes claims for common concerns on social, economic, and cultural fronts, despite the obvious differences between and within member nations. Offering a way of looking beyond these inherent inconsistencies, Sinah Theres Kloß argues that the Global South "has to be understood as something that is created, imagined, invented, maintained, and recreated."[15] The Global South is thus best understood as an "imagined community"—not a nation, but a community of nations sharing similar (though not identical) experiences of decolonization and unequal economic development. In the digital age, this community-building happens not only in physical streets or urban complexes but also in online spaces. One of the things that this collection explores therefore is how digital Shakespeares speak to some of these common concerns of the Global South; and how in turn a study of digital Shakespeares helps us better understand the growing communities of the Global South.

---

[13] Lalwani, "Tech savvy Indians drive to villages for Covid-19 vaccinations."

[14] Mahapatra, "Digital divide will exclude marginalised from jabs: Supreme Court."

[15] Kloß, 7.

WHOSE DIGITAL SHAKESPEARE IS IT ANYWAY?

To speak of the digital is to acknowledge a heterogeneous space with differing levels of technical competence, bandwidth, and participation. British Council's "Mix the Play" for instance, was also pitched as an educational platform, an extension of the organization's aim to promote English language and literature globally. "Mix the Play" made its appearance in Indian schools as well as higher educational institutions as part of student competitions and festivals.[16] British Council Bangladesh in its website similarly lists the interactive gaming platform under "Our work in arts, education, and society."[17] While the ease with which the British Council can market its digital educational and entertainment tools, including but not restricted to "Mix the Play" suggests a growing population of young tech-savvy users in the Global South, digital literacy itself cannot be assumed to be universal. For instance, less privileged schools would not have the bandwidth or equipment to enable their students to play the game online. Then again, "Mix the Play" assumes an audience well versed in English, which would be true of elite and usually urban populations of the Global South. In rural schools and colleges, many catering to first generation learners, English would not be the medium of instruction, even while teaching Shakespeare. British Council India's decision to host the interactive platform at IKBF thus might be seen as an exercise in digital outreach, an attempt to bring digital tools to a wider cross-section of the population that might not have worked completely.

Speaking of the now familiar catch-word, the "digital divide," Massimo Ragnedda and Anna Gladkova alert us to different levels of disparity. They argue that with the rise of the internet in the Global South, the first level of the digital divide based on raw access to Information and Communications Technology (ICTs) has been shrinking. This, however, has led to "new forms of inequalities" or a second level of digital divide within the region based on technological access, gender, educational levels, economic empowerment, and digital skills.[18] A further third level of the digital divide arises from "the different capacity/ability to fully

---

[16] British Council India. "British Council presents 'Shakespeare Mela' at BITS Pilani Pearl Festival."

[17] British Council Bangladesh. "Mix the Play."

[18] Ragnedda and Gladkova, "Introduction," 1–2.

exploit the Internet and to transform its use into tangible outcomes."[19] While differences in digital skill and access might exist anywhere in the world, in the Global South they are symptoms of a digital revolution that is still unfolding.[20] This has implications not only for digital projects and platforms but also for critical scholarship on digital cultures. Calling for the need to recognize the "global shift [in the internet revolution] with distinct yet connected histories and inevitably different trajectories, meanings, and effects,"[21] Aswin Punathambekar and Sriram Mohan urge for the need to "combat the universalizing tendencies of Anglo-American discourse" in the study of digital cultures.[22] What is needed, therefore, is for critical attention to be turned toward these new digital spaces.

The Global South has its own distinct set of relations with digital resources that need to be understood in their own right. For instance, large swathes of cutting edge critical scholarship remain unavailable to scholars from the Global South since universities and public libraries are unable to match levels of subscriptions of the institutions of the Global North. During the pandemic, in recognition of this disparity, some presses and online repositories started special access coupons and options for researchers specifically from the Global South, but these remain limited. In terms of online instruction, for instance, in the absence of Learning Management Systems (LMS) other than Google Classroom, it was WhatsApp an instant messaging and Voice over Internet Protocol (VoIP) service that became the most popular educational tool in Africa and Asia.[23] The relatively low-tech requirements of WhatsApp made it easier for students and faculty to communicate and share resources via their phones. Videos, messages, as well as document files can be shared to individuals as well as designated groups, making asynchronous learning possible. To speak of digital Shakespeares in the Global South, especially

---

[19] Ragnedda and Gladkova, 2.

[20] See for instance Punathambekar and Mohan "Introduction: Mapping Global Digital Cultures," 2–3.

[21] Punathambekar and Mohan, 2–3.

[22] Punathambekar and Mohan, 4.

[23] For more on the extensive usage of WhatsApp as an educational tool see Madge et al., "WhatsApp use among African international distance education (IDE) students;" Mwareya and Simango, "How an 'unqualified' 27-year-old Zimbabwean teacher created a top tutoring academy on WhatsApp."

during the pandemic, is to thus imagine *Macbeth* being taught on WhatsApp. But it is also to imagine remarkable pre-pandemic productions such as *Romeo and Juliet Separated by War* (2015) directed by exiled Syrian actor Nawar Bulbul that was made possible by and got played out on Skype.[24] With two sets of cast, one comprising Syrian refugee children from a hospital in Jordan, and the other of children who remained in warn-torn Homs, Syria, rehearsals as well as the final performances were all carried out in makeshift theaters via Skype. Highlighting the vagaries of live digital performances in conflict zones of the Global South, audiences for one of the shows, had to wait for an hour for the balcony scene until the internet feed from Syria was re-established.[25]

Questions of access apart, the internet is, of course, not a neutral space. As Lisa Nakamura famously declared in *Cybertypes*: "The Internet is a place where race happens."[26] The racialization of the internet begins at the level of code and algorithms (how for instance search engines conflate certain names but can recognize others), and continues through different stages of usage. At the same time, as Ayanna Thompson and Ruben Espinosa have shown, digital Shakespeares can provide an important platform for exploring, performing, and broadcasting oneself, especially amongst students belonging to minority communities.[27] Web platforms such as YouTube can become important archives for amateur as well as professional performances that would otherwise be lost. Digital initiatives like the *World Shakespeare Project* or *The Tsikinya-Chaka Centre* can also provide important tools for cross-cultural exchange, bringing together communities from different parts of the world who would otherwise be unable to connect. Moreover, open access performance archives such as *MIT Global Shakespeares*, and *Asian Shakespeare Intercultural Archive* (A|S|I|A), or even digital projects such as *Shakespeare in Bengal* play a fundamental role in archiving and making globally available the local productions, pedagogic materials as well as Shakespeare ephemera from the Global South. As Judy Celine Ick observes, however, digital archives and platforms are not without challenges: not all regions or

---

[24] British Library, "Photographs of a Syrian Romeo and Juliet, 2015."

[25] Agence France-Presse, "Skype Meets Theatre in Syria Twist on Romeo and Juliet."

[26] Nakamura, *Cybertypes*, xi.

[27] Thompson. "Unmooring the Moor: Researching and Teaching on YouTube;" Espinosa, "Beyond The Tempest: Language, Legitimacy, and La Frontera."

communities for instance get equal representation and not everyone might have the bandwidth to screen these performances.[28] These challenges are not unique to Shakespeare but are characteristic of Digital Humanities projects. Addressing this question head-on, and drawing on Black Feminism, Roopika Risam, advocates an intersectional digital humanities: "foregrounding difference and resisting flattening of specificities that emerge from practice," she argues, "offers useful guidance for attending to the tension between local and global articulations of digital humanities."[29]

This collection takes into account the larger questions of critical inclusiveness and intersectionality that global new media scholars like Risam and Punathambekar highlight. The chapters in this collection attempt to capture the diversity of digital Shakespeares from the Global South, both in terms of medium and region. The "Rhizomatic Bard," a term coined by Maurizio Calbi and Stephen O'Neill,[30] expanding upon Douglas Lanier's framework of "Shakespearean rhizomatics,"[31] is particularly helpful in thinking about digital Shakespeares within a broader global perspective. The Deleuzoguattarian rhizome, by replacing a hierarchical arboreal structure, allows us to further consider these plural global appropriations by de-centering Shakespeare whether they be performances in Stratford or London or digital production or pedagogy from the Global North. The chapters that follow cover a wide cross-section of geographies, exploring how digital media and Shakespeare come together in the Global South. Many of the chapters were written during the Covid-19 pandemic, and address the exacerbated problems of digital access and participation that came to the forefront during this time. As the chapters make clear, however, issues related to digitization in the Global South did not come into being as a result of the pandemic, and will likely continue even after the crisis is over.

Starting us off with the big stakes questions, Heidi Craig and Laura Estill's chapter "Finding and Accessing Shakespeare Scholarship in the

---

[28] Ick, "The Performance Archive and the Digital Construction of Asian Shakespeare," n.p.

[29] Risam, "Navigating the Global Digital Humanities: Insights from Black Feminism," n.p.

[30] Calbi and O'Neill. "Introduction: #SocialmediaShakespeares."

[31] Lanier, "Shakespearean Rhizomatics: Adaptation, Ethics, Value."

Global South: Digital Research and Bibliography" highlights the problems of visibility of scholarly research that is produced outside of the Global North. Turning to the inequities of access, Craig and Estill underscore the importance of "listening" to the scholarship from the Global South. As they argue even before the establishment of Global Shakespeares as a field in critical studies, people from different parts of the world have been writing about Shakespeare. These texts, however, are often available only in regional languages, thus making them invisible to dominant Anglo-American critical traditions. What lies at stake is the recognition of academic labor from the Global South by way of citation as well as the expansion of our critical conversations. Craig and Estill explore how digital tools, especially digital repositories and bibliographies such as *World Shakespeare Bibliography* can help counter some of these apparent gaps or silences in the critical archive. Chris Thurman's "From 'English Never Loved Us' to JAM at the Windybrow: Covid-era Digital Shakespeares in/from South Africa" examines the different digital initiatives in South Africa that used Shakespeare during the pandemic. Turning to specific examples such as the Pendoring Advertising Awards' "English Never Loved Us" campaign, online performance initiatives like the Market Theatre's "Chilling with the Bard" series and #lockdownshakespeare, the chapter shows how a wide range of both incidental and detailed appropriations of Shakespeare arose shortly after the onset of the pandemic. The result, Thurman argues, is what might best be described as fragmented "bitesize Shakespeares." These "bitesize Shakespeares," however, provided a powerful counter-narrative to the traditional "weighty" Shakespeares of South African school curriculum that were inflected by colonial history.

In "Practicing Digital Shakespeare in Latin America: case studies from Argentina and Brazil" Amrita Sen looks at two distinct but connected websites—*Fundación Shakespeare Argentina* and the "Shakespeare in Brazil" section of the *MIT Global Shakespeares*—that are aimed at making globally accessible the performances and textual translations from Latin America. Sen argues that these websites open up new possibilities of decolonial community-building through their curatorial strategies and social outreach. They not only act as repositories of actual performances, but also function as archives of communal memories. In "Teaching Shakespeare in the Indian (Google) Classroom: The Digital Promise and the Digital Divide" Souvik Mukherjee turns to questions of digital divide and access in the Indian classroom. He situates digital learning within the context of Shakespeare pedagogy in India beginning with Thomas Babington Macaulay's infamous "Minute" (1835) that helped re-design the Indian education system. While traditional Shakespeare teaching in Indian schools and universities valorized the individual professors turning them into larger than life figures, the digital age has prompted the transition to a more democratic model. Simultaneously, the changes in classroom pedagogy have led to a greater utilization of scholarly websites such as *MIT Global Shakespeares*. Despite its democratic potential, however, digital learning still remains accessible to mainly urban and privileged groups. Mukherjee's chapter thus explores how existing digital inequities have been exacerbated by the pandemic, and where Shakespeare fits into the "brave new world" of online teaching in India.

As Alexa Alice Joubin powerfully notes in her afterword, Shakespeare has become a "digital nomad." If in the previous centuries Shakespeare had been a "cultural nomad" shifting from one geography to the next through performances, translations, and adaptations, then with the onset of new technologies, especially in the wake of the pandemic, the bard is now a "digital nomad." Highlighting the growth of global Shakespeares as a cultural movement as well as an industry, Joubin observes how "the digital sphere" has become its "most important habitation." Charting these technological changes Joubin focuses on two in particular—screening interface and digital archival practices—to show how these affect the Global South and the Global North differently. Archives, including digital ones, are not only impacted by memories and problems of access, but also by censorship. The afterword thus interrogates the politics of digital technologies and the ways in which they shape our understanding of the Global South as well as the growing field of global Shakespeares.

Digital Shakespeares from the Global South pushes the boundaries of what we understand as the role of the bard in digital culture. As the chapters in this collection show, despite geographical variations and differing cultural contexts, the Global South shares several common elements when it comes to digital Shakespeares. Questions of access remain in the foreground, whether in terms of raw availability of the internet as Mukherjee shows, or the problems of accessing scholarship and adaptations that Craig and Estill, and Joubin highlight. And yet, digital Shakespeares in the Global South remain full of possibilities, forging new community connections, and coming up with innovative, often radical, uses of existing technology to meet challenges of infrastructure. What Thurman,

Sen, and Mukherjee reveal are the ways in which performances, peda-gogic practices, websites, and repositories adapt not only Shakespeare, but also digital technologies to their unique needs. As we renew our engagement with Shakespeare adaptations globally amidst a pandemic, these plural voices in the digital landscape become all the more impor-tant. We are in the middle of a digital turn in literary studies, precipitated by the closure of universities and theaters—phenomena that would seem uncannily familiar to scholars of Shakespeare and the early modern period. Our understanding of Shakespeare's nomadic journeys in digital space would necessitate an inclusion of other digital geographies and practices. This collection offers a new set of readings that expand our parameters of studying Shakespeare, and Shakespeare appropriations globally.

References

Agence France-Presse. "Skype Meets Theatre in Syria Twist on Romeo and Juliet." NDTV. April 6, 2015. https://gadgets.ndtv.com/internet/features/skype-meets-theatre-in-syria-twist-on-romeo-and-juliet-678190.

British Council. *Mix the Play: Romeo and Juliet*, dir. Roysten Abel. https://mix theplay.britishcouncil.org/. Accessed May 26, 2021.

British Council Bangladesh. "Mix the Play." https://www.britishcouncil.org.bd/en/programmes/shakespeare-lives/mix-the-play. Accessed September 22, 2021.

British Council India. "British Council Presents 'Shakespeare Mela' at BITS Pilani Pearl Festival." https://www.britishcouncil.in/about/press/british-council-presents-%E2%80%98shakespeare-mela%E2%80%99-bits-pilani-pearl-festival Accessed September 22, 2021.

British Library. "Photographs of a Syrian Romeo and Juliet, 2015." https://www.bl.uk/collection-items/photographs-of-a-syrian-romeo-and-juliet-2015. Accessed October 2, 2021.

Calbi, Maurizio and Stephen O'Neill. "Introduction: #SocialmediaShakespeares." Special issue on Shakespeare and Social Media. *Borrowers and Lenders: The Journal of Shakespeare and Appropriation*. Volume X.1.

Carson, Christie and Peter Kirwan. "Shakespeare and the Digital World Intro-duction." *Shakespeare and the Digital World*. Ed. Christie Carson and Peter Kirwan. Cambridge: Cambridge University Press, 2014.

Dirlik, Arif. "Global South: Predicament and Promise." *The Global South* Vol. 1, No. 1 (Winter, 2007), pp. 12–23.

Espinosa, Ruben. "Beyond The Tempest: Language, Legitimacy, and La Fron-tera." *The Shakespeare User: Critical and Creative Appropriations in a*

Networked Culture. Ed. Valerie M. Fazel, Louise Geddes. New York: Palgrave Macmillan, 2017.

Fazel, Valerie M. and Louise Geddes. "Introduction: The Shakespeare User." *The Shakespeare User: Critical and Creative Appropriations in a Networked Culture*. Ed. Valerie M. Fazel and Louise Geddes. New York: Palgrave Macmillan, 2017.

Ghosh, Bishwanath. "Kolkata book fair put off due to COVID-19." *The Hindu*. January 7, 2021. https://www.thehindu.com/news/cities/kolkata/kolkata-book-fair-put-off-due-to-covid-19/article33518030.ece.

Ick, Judy Celine. "The Performance Archive and the Digital Construction of Asian Shakespeare." *Asian Interventions in Global Shakespeare: 'All the World's His Stage'*. Poonam Trivedi, Paromita Chakravarti, Ted Motohashi. London: Routledge, 2020. Epub.

Kloß, Sinah Theres. "The Global South as Subversive Practice: Challenges and Potentials of a Heuristic Concept," *The Global South*, Vol. 11, No. 2 (Fall 2017), pp. 1–17.

Kullman, Thomas. "Shakespeare on the Internet: Global and South Asian Appropriations." *Asian Interventions in Global Shakespeare: 'All the World's His Stage'*. Ed. Poonam Trivedi, Paromita Chakravarti, and Ted Motohashi. London: Routledge, 2020. Epub.

Lalwani, Vijayta. "Tech savvy Indians drive to villages for Covid-19 vaccinations. Those without smartphones lose out." Scroll.in. May 17, 2021. https://scroll.in/article/994871/tech-savvy-indians-drive-to-villages-for-covid-19-vaccinations-those-without-smartphones-lose-out.

Lanier, Douglas. 2014. "Shakespearean Rhizomatics: Adaptation, Ethics, Value." *Shakespeare and the Ethics of Appropriation*. Ed. Alexa Huang and Elizabeth Rivlin. New York: Palgrave Macmillan. Kindle.

Levander, Caroline and Walter Mignolo. "Introduction: The Global South and World Dis/Order," *The Global South*, Vol. 5, No. 1 (Spring 2011), pp. 1–11.

Madge, Clare, et al. "WhatsApp use among African international distance education (IDE) students: transferring, translating and transforming educational experiences." *Learning, Media and Technology*. Vol. 44, No. 3 (2019). https://www.tandfonline.com/doi/full/10.1080/17439884.2019.1628048.

Mahapatra, Dhananjay. "Digital Divide will Exclude Marginalised from Jabs: Supreme Court." The Times of India. June 3, 2021. https://timesofindia.indiatimes.com/india/digital-divide-will-exclude-marginalised-from-jabs-supreme-court/articleshow/83185732.cms.

Mignolo, Walter. *The Darker Side of Western Modernity: Global Futures, Decolonial Options*. [1995]. Durham: Duke University Press, 2011.

Minami, Ryuta. "What's in a Name? Shakespeare and Japanese Pop Culture." *The Routledge Handbook of Shakespeare and Global Appropriation*. Ed. Christy Desmet, Sujata Iyengar, and Miriam Jacobson. New York: Routledge, 2020.

Mwareya, Ray and Audrey Simango. "How an "Unqualified" 27-Year-Old Zimbabwean Teacher Created a Top Tutoring Academy on WhatsApp." Rest of the World. June 25, 2021. https://restofworld.org/2021/learning-on-the-last-mile/.

Punathambekar Aswin and Sriram Mohan. "Introduction: Mapping Global Digital Cultures." *Global Digital Cultures: Perspectives from South Asia*. Ed. Aswin Punathambekar and Sriram Mohan. Ann Arbor: University of Michigan Press, 2019.

Ragnedda, Massimo and Anna Gladkova. "Introduction." *Digital Inequalities in the Global South*. Ed. Massimo Ragnedda and Anna Gladkova. New York: Palgrave Macmillan, 2020.

Risam, Roopika. "Navigating the Global Digital Humanities: Insights from Black Feminism." *Debates in the Digital Humanities 2016*. Ed. Matthew K. Gold and Lauren F. Klein. Minneapolis: University of Minnesota Press, 2016. Epub.

Thompson, Ayanna. "Unmooring the Moor: Researching and Teaching on YouTube." *Shakespeare Quarterly*, Vol. 61, No. 3 (Fall 2010), pp. 337–356.

Young, Sandra. *Shakespeare in the Global South: Stories of Oceans Crossed in Contemporary Adaptation*. Bloomsbury, 2019.

CHAPTER 2

Finding and Accessing Shakespeare Scholarship in the Global South: Digital Research and Bibliography

Heidi Craig and Laura Estill

Abstract There was a time when articles about Shakespeare were published around the globe, but few knew where to find them all. Shakespeare studies thrived in non-Anglophone countries in the Global South: articles appeared in regional journals, institutional bulletins, and society newsletters, each of which might have a publication run of only a few dozen copies. This chapter traces the move from regionalized Shakespeare publication to truly global publication. It considers how online publishing (including open journal systems and open-access publishing), institutional repositories, and digital bibliography make research from

H. Craig (✉)
Texas A&M University, College Station, TX, USA
e-mail: hcraig@tamu.edu

L. Estill
St. Francis Xavier University, Antigonish, NS, Canada
e-mail: lestill@stfx.ca

© The Author(s) 2022
A. Sen (ed.), *Digital Shakespeares from the Global South*,
Global Shakespeares, https://doi.org/10.1007/978-3-031-04787-9_2

around the Globe findable. This chapter examines how the *World Shakespeare Bibliography* participates in global Shakespeare studies by making multilingual criticism, editions, and performances searchable.

Keywords *World Shakespeare Bibliography* · Online Bibliographies and repositories · Visibility of scholarship from Global South

In "Shakespeare Comes to Indonesia," Michael Skupin discusses Trisno Sumardjo's English-to-Indonesian Shakespeare translations from the early 1950s. Sumardjo's translations—including *Hamlet, Pangeran Denmark*, and *Saudagar Venezia* [*The Merchant of Venice*], both published in 1950—drew from both the original English texts and from Dutch-language translations of Shakespeare's plays, the latter reflecting the legacy of the Netherlands' colonization of Indonesia.[1] For many of Sumardjo's Indonesian readers in the 1950s, Dutch was "the language of advantage in pre-independence Indonesia,"[2] its apparent cultural capital dovetailing with Shakespeare's international reputation as a global literary icon (a status itself steeped in long histories of English cultural, economic and political imperialism). Sumardjo made Shakespeare available in the "local" language (as opposed to the "language of advantage") but not before filtering the text through the colonial language imposed on that locality. Sumardjo's Shakespeare translations, then, exemplify many of the complexities of Global Shakespeare: an English-language play is translated into a local language, by way of another language introduced by colonizers. Indonesian translations of Shakespeare grant local populations agency over documents historically imposed on them. Through translation, global audiences make Shakespeare their own, shrugging off imposed languages along with other forms of colonial domination. At the same time, these translations can maintain the whiff of colonial oppression, reifying a system of value that prizes the culture of colonial powers, and crowds out local voices.

Sumardjo's 1950s translations also speak to the fact that, long before "Global Shakespeare(s)" was a named field, global Shakespeare studies

---

[1] Indonesia proclaimed independence from the Netherlands in 1946; the United Nations recognized Indonesia as a sovereign nation in 1949.

[2] Skupin, "Shakespeare Comes to Indonesia," 101.

were carried out around the world. Skupin, a teacher of Chinese Culture University in Taipei, published "Shakespeare Comes to Indonesia" in *Multicultural Shakespeare: Translation, Appropriation and Performance*, a journal devoted to global Shakespeares published by University of Łódź in Poland and De Gruyter, and edited by Kawachi Yoshiko from Kyorin University and Krystyna Kujawińska Courtney from the University of Łódź.[3] The editors themselves are active scholars in Global Shakespeare studies: Yoshiko has published on the reception of Shakespeare in modern Japan, while Kujawińska Courtney is a leader in the study of the reception of Shakespeare in Poland and has also co-edited *The Globalization of Shakespeare in the Nineteenth Century*. As this brief introductory example suggests, the translation, research, and publication of Shakespeare is a global affair, leading to collaboration between scholars across continents, past and present. Shakespeare studies have thrived around the world, in the Global North and South, in Anglophone and non-Anglophone countries alike, for decades and in many cases, centuries.

And yet, while the wealth of research produced in different regions such as the Global South is unmistakable, the ability to *find* and *access* this scholarship can range wildly depending on one's region.[4] Articles might appear in regional journals, institutional bulletins, and society newsletters, each of which might have a publication run of only a few dozen copies. In that case, few scholars outside the immediate area could know what existed or be able to access research from a given location. This speaks to a too-often undervalued fact about scholarly discourse: while publication is undoubtedly important for disseminating research, equally important is retrieval and access. Only once these are in place, regionalized Shakespeare studies can become truly global. The digital turn has made Global Shakespeares more accessible: open-access journals like *Multicultural Shakespeare* contribute to an academic study of Shakespeare that is truly global in scope.

This chapter contributes to a collection on Shakespeare in the Global South by considering how we find and access scholarship from around the world often without even leaving our homes. Having much of the world at our fingertips beneath our keys, does not, however, mean

---

[3] For more on *Multicultural Shakespeare*, see https://czasopisma.uni.lodz.pl/szekspir/about.

[4] For more on systemic barriers to knowledge production facing scholars in the Global South, see Márton Demeter, *Academic Knowledge Production and the Global South*.

that we can find or access materials equally. As we demonstrate, online publishing (including open journal systems and open-access publishing), digital databases, repositories, and digital bibliography make Shakespearean research from around the world findable. From the scores of digital resources from particular locales, regions, or countries which aggregate and disseminate Shakespeare research and performance, we discuss the *South Asian Review of English*; the Shakespeare Society of Eastern India; the journal *Shakespeare in Southern Africa*; and the KL Shakespeare Players from Kuala Lumpur, together representing a range of approaches, "traditional" and innovative, democratizing and elevating Shakespeare's global reach. These complement digital resources committed to a pan-regional or pan-Global approach, such as the Asian Shakespeare Intercultural Archive (A|S|I|A), MIT's Global Shakespeares, *Multicultural Shakespeares, Borrowers and Lenders*, and the *World Shakespeare Bibliography* (*WSB*). Together, these local, global, and glocal digital resources participate in global Shakespeare studies by making international and multilingual criticism, editions, and performances available and searchable.[5] Digital publication can enable finding scholarship by and about the Global South; it can also enable access for scholars working in the Global South.

With this essay, we seek to acknowledge the lack of visibility of Shakespeare scholars from the Global South, particularly due to a dearth of citation, and to contribute to its remedy through a citation practice that moves beyond the typical centres of Shakespeare studies.[6] Shakespeare scholarship, as it currently stands, is dominated by Anglo-America and the well-funded institutions and publishing mechanisms that help make this scholarship visible. The problem of accessibility not only leaves scholars of the Global South invisible to those outside of those regional or linguistic communities, but also raises obstacles to any aspirations of South-South cooperation. Citing scholarship of the Global South can contribute to a positive feedback loop of further citation and increased visibility for scholars who have been historically and undeservedly marginalized within the field.

Digital publishing can offer the promise of democratizing both the production of knowledge and access to that knowledge, yet, as this

---

[5] Craig, ed., *World Shakespeare Bibliography*, www.worldshakesbib.org.

[6] See Demeter on "citation universes," 164–65 and passim.

chapter recognizes, online publishing tends only to reinforce existing power dynamics. We consider challenges that face scholars working in languages other than English, and the difficulties that arise when it comes to considering global Shakespeare journal articles. We conclude by showing how digital resources not only publish research on global Shakespeare; they participate in the act of global Shakespeare studies.

Building on important work on the history of global Shakespeare studies, particularly with regards to scholarship on performance and reception, this chapter focuses on Shakespearean publication in the broad sense of "making public," as registered in exhibitions, online pedagogical performances, scholarly periodicals in the form of journals and journal articles, and bibliographies. Our broad approach is informed by Alexa Alice Joubin's argument that we need to transform "global Shakespeares from centerpieces in exotic displays into critical methodologies."[7] Focusing on the performance archive, Joubin tackles the "archival silences" in global Shakespeare studies that "place entire avenues of thought beyond our research."[8] Drawing on Joubin, this chapter turns to the archive of Shakespeare studies as registered in multilingual journal articles published around the world. Archival silences can be the consequence of redaction or now-lost information, which can be difficult to overcome. But they can also result from lack of access and findability, problems which digital resources can help rectify, yet too often exacerbate.[9] Some of the most glaring silences in the archive of journal articles about Shakespeare have been work by non-Western and non-Anglophone scholars. Moreover, what scholars from the Global North deem as "silence" or "gaps" can actually be a matter of their failure to recognize or attend to ongoing conversations. Effective research is a matter of learning where to look and how to listen.

We come to this article as two white Anglophone scholars from the Global North. We were invited to write this article based on our editorship of the *World Shakespeare Bibliography* (Craig is editor, Estill is past editor), a digital resource whose purview includes the goal of making Shakespeare resources from around the world, including the Global South, findable for scholars. When we began this chapter, we were tasked

[7] Joubin, "Global Shakespeares as Methodology," 274.

[8] Joubin, "Global Shakespeares as Methodology," 284.

[9] Gil, "Through the Breaking-Glass," esp. around 17:00.

with writing about global Shakespeare, yet, as we demonstrate, "global Shakespeare" is always the study of particulars rooted in different cultures and geographies. As this chapter explores, supporting "global Shakespeare studies" with projects such as the *World Shakespeare Bibliography* will only be fruitful if we continue to produce, study, and engage with Shakespeare locally, as chapters by Chris Thurman, Amrita Sen, and Souvik Mukherjee demonstrate. We do not presume to speak for the Global South; rather, our chapter considers how we can best listen. As we articulate, improved enumerative bibliography, both on the global scale with the *World Shakespeare Bibliography* and on local scales, as well as access to publications (both digital projects and journal articles) is one of the ways to amplify previously muted scholarship in order to facilitate a truly global approach to Shakespeare.

GLOBAL SHAKESPEARES BEFORE "GLOBAL SHAKESPEARES"

A search for "Global Shakespeare*"[10] in the *World Shakespeare Bibliography* (*WSB*) brings up only a few results before the year 2000, including an annotation for a journal article from 1989 that discusses "the global Shakespeare industry,"[11] the MIT *Global Shakespeares* site,[12] and a "Global Shakespeare" book series by International Thomson Publishing launched in 1997.[13] At the turn of the twenty-first century, however, we see the term "Global Shakespeare" begin to be widely adopted. Of course, Shakespeare studies, translations, and performances existed around the world well before the "global Shakespeare" label or critical approach was used; in other words, the practice of global Shakespeare predates "Global Shakespeare(s)" as a recognized field of study.[14] Before "global

---

[10] In *The World Shakespeare Bibliography*, an asterisk is a wildcard that can "represent one or more variable characters." This search was done with quotation marks so that the word Global had to be directly before the word Shakespeare (phrase searching). For more on searching the *WSB*, see worldshakesbib.org/search-help.

[11] Liechtenstein, "Is Shakespeare Still Our Contemporary?"; *WSB* entry bf1548.

[12] Donaldson, ed., *Global Shakespeares*, globalshakespeares.mit.edu.

[13] For some of the volumes in this series, see *WSB* av139, av140, and av141.

[14] For a history and state-of-the-field of "Global Shakespeare," see Desmet, Iyengar, and Jacobson, eds, *The Routledge Handbook of Shakespeare and Global Appropriation* and Joubin, Vyroubalova, and Pentland, eds, *The Palgrave Encyclopedia of Global Shakespeare*, particularly Joubin, "Global Shakespeares: A Critical Introduction."

Shakespeare" was a named field, scholars published about Shakespeare in international journals. These journals were often associated with a particular society, university, or region; they might be published in English or regional languages. Just as we have global Shakespeares plural—consider the name of MIT's *Global Shakespeares*, an important digital resource—this field has plural histories, rather than a single, unified history, which involves performance, translation, adaptation, reception, tourism, and scholarship.

For instance, in response to a British Council-sponsored Shakespeare exhibition in Kuala Lumpur, Malaysia in 1980, Ooi Boo Eng's essay-in-verse, "For 'The Age of Shakespeare' Exhibition," (1981) invokes Shakespeare's transhistorical and trans-cultural cultural dominance which is at once both impressive and problematic. Anxiety about Shakespeare's tendency to eclipse others is not unique to the modern Global South: Eng cites the sixteenth-century dramatist Robert Greene's envious resentment of his contemporary Shakespeare, exemplified by Greene's memorable insult of Shakespeare as the "upstart crow"; addressing Shakespeare, the poem imagines Greene's reaction to Shakespeare's status: "A fit, now, he would throw / to see you, world-wide, an industry, supporting many a professor's salary."[15] As the essay-in-verse suggests, since the sixteenth century Shakespeare's reputation has not only grown steadily upward but also outward, becoming the centre of a global industry supporting academics and artists, and potentially a symbol of political, economic, and cultural imperialism. As its title indicates, Eng's essay-in-verse was occasioned by the "Age of Shakespeare" Exhibition in Kuala Lumpur in October 1980, sponsored by the British Council. The event prompts a meditation on Shakespeare and the English language as a celebrated yet ambivalent legacy of a colonial power on the wane:

> What's England coming to
> these days?
> With one voice the world says:
> Gone to seed but for two
> very English things:
> English and you, Shakespeare,
> dramatist without peer
> (and perhaps the British Council, too).

[15] Eng, "For 'The Age of Shakespeare' Exhibition," 63.

In this poem, the presence of Shakespeare offers an uneasy reminder of the British colonization of the Malay Peninsula, but also fodder for local populations to appropriate and remake into their own, and which sparks global Shakespeare studies. "For 'The Age of Shakespeare' Exhibition" appeared in an early issue of *The South Asian Review of English* (*SARE*), a journal devoted to critical conversations "from all of the world," "on the literatures, languages, and cultures of Southeast, South, and East Asia." From its outset, *SARE* has ranged beyond South Asia in terms of subject matter: following its inaugural publication in 1980, early issues included "A Guide to Canadian Fiction"[16] as well as attention to the literature of New Zealand. Existing solely as an electronic journal from 2016, *SARE* has digitized all of its early issues, making them available open access and readable from abroad.

A recent issue of *SARE* features Su Mei Kok's "'What's Past is Prologue': Postcolonialism, Globalisation, and the Demystification of Shakespeare in Malaysia," which considers the impact of KL Shakespeare, a Kuala-Lumpur-based theatre troupe, within the context of globalized education. With a motto that "Shakespeare was originally written not to be studied by intellectuals or seen by snobs, but to be performed for the general masses,"[17] KL Shakespeare's pedagogical production series "Shakespeare Demystified," is designed to make Shakespeare accessible to new audiences who might typically be intimidated by Shakespeare's language. Their stated goal is "to take Shakespeare to every state in Malaysia, and eventually to all countries in Southeast Asia."[18] In 2017, KL Shakespeare performed *Macbeth* across Malaysia and overseas in Manila and Seoul. Their pedagogical outreach extends beyond performance, and indeed beyond the playhouse: In 2021, the KL Shakespeare Players (KLSP) received a British Council "Connecting Through Culture" grant: over a series of workshops on "objects in Shakespeare" the KLSP "will be exploring how to transform these 'things' playfully in productions for non-native English-speaking children." During the COVID-19 pandemic, KL Shakespeare continued to perform and engage their audiences with live interactive online shows, performing 50 online shows in 2020 and continuing into 2021, with a performance

---

16 New, "A Guide to Canadian Fiction."

17 KL Shakespeare, http://www.klshakespeare.com.my/about-us.

18 KL Shakespeare, http://www.klshakespeare.com.my/about-us.

of *King Lear*. KL Shakespeare's "Shakespeare Demystified," was originally designed to make English-language Shakespearean performances
accessible to audiences across South East Asia; their online ticketed performances in the COVID-19 era make Shakespeare accessible in a different
way.[19]

The *South Asian Review of English* is one of several regional journals which has contributed to the study of Shakespeare in and of the
Global South, as part of its wider study of literatures across the globe.
Similarly, *Theatre International*, the annual journal of the Shakespeare
Society of Eastern India, publishes Shakespeare criticism amid a broader
approach.[20] Its inaugural volume, titled "East West Perspectives on
Theatre" published in 1994, announced *Theatre International* as "an
international Journal-cum-Dramabook" which intends to "cater to the
frontierless international community" of scholars and artists through "the
constitution of its editorial board, through its intended wide-angle global
readership, in its range and scope of subject matter and focus, in its
selection of experts and specialist writers."[21] Though not devoted to
Shakespeare exclusively, *Theatre International*'s description of its mission
is an apt manifesto for Global Shakespeares publication. Aimed at a
wide international audience in 1994, the online publication of this
journal makes the work still more accessible to a broader audience of
Shakespeareans. Again, all this speaks to the importance of access for
disseminating Shakespeare scholarship.

SARE and *Theatre International* respectively embed Shakespeare
within their broad approaches to literature and theatre. Regional journals
exclusively devoted to Shakespeare also play a crucial role. *Shakespeare in
Southern Africa* is a project of the Shakespeare Society of Southern Africa,
and published as part of *African Journals Online*, which is committed to
open access. Although its title suggests a tight focus on Shakespeare in a
particular region, its geographical scope is international. They are particularly interested in Shakespeare's impact in the Global South: inviting

---

[19] KL Shakespeare, http://www.klshakespeare.com.my/about-us. See also the forthcoming issue of *Early Modern Digital Review* on "Digital Representations of Contemporary Shakespeare Performances," ed. Bi-Qi Beatrice Lei, https://jps.library.utoronto.ca/
index.php/emdr.

[20] This journal is available open access at: https://ssei.org.in/journal.html.

[21] Amitava Roy et al., ed, *Theatre International*, https://www.ssei.org.in/TI/VOL%
20I.pdf.

contributions discussing the legacy of Shakespeare throughout Africa, with a specific focus on the Shakespearean experience in particular African countries. In addition, the journal "actively seeks to publish articles investigating the impact of Shakespeare in other parts of the world, such as India, the United States, South East Asia and South America."[22] Even seemingly regional journals, then, can be committed to and undertake pan-global approaches to Shakespeare. Digitization of decades' worth of the *South Asian Review of English, Shakespeare in Southern Africa*, and *Theatre International* of the Shakespeare Society of Eastern India demonstrates the importance of dissemination, often digital, of traditional scholarship in the form of academic journals.

Geographically or regionally focused Shakespeare journals are complemented by the wide coverage of journals like *Multicultural Shakespeare* and *Borrowers and Lenders*. Open-access online journals allow for research to be shared more easily across the globe: print-only journals have a limited circulation and paywalled journals might only be available to academics working at universities which can afford to subscribe to them. Subscription budgets for humanities journals and bibliographies vary and each country faces different accessibility problems. Although online journals also have barriers to access, they make information available to anyone with an internet connection.

Multicultural Shakespeare: Translation, Appropriation, and Performance, published by Łódź University Press, is a print and open-access online journal that is devoted to the study of Global Shakespeare. *Multicultural Shakespeare* solicits contributions from "researchers, especially those from non-English-speaking backgrounds...that contribute to the creation and understanding of Shakespeare as [a] global phenomenon."[23] Their recent special issues have included "Shakespeare, Blackface, and Performance: A Global Exploration" (2020), "Shakespeare and Intermedial / Cross-Cultural Contacts" (2019), and "Shakespeare, National Origins, and Nationality" (2016). *Multicultural Shakespeare* is a model of online Global Shakespeare Studies because of its commitment to publishing diverse academic voices and representing research about "local concerns."[24] It is precisely this journal's emphasis on local interpretations

---

[22] *Shakespeare in Southern Africa*, https://www.ajol.info/index.php/sisa.

[23] https://czasopisma.uni.lodz.pl/szekspir/issue/archive.

[24] Ibid.

of Shakespeare that contributes to Global Shakespeare, the catch-all name we apply to the polyvocal and multi-focused study of particulars.

As their title suggests, *Borrowers and Lenders: The Journal of Shakespeare and Appropriation*, from the University of Georgia in the United States, another open-access online Shakespeare journal, focuses on adaptations and appropriation. This area of focus actively invites scholars working on Global Shakespeare, as many articles about Global Shakespeare focus on translation, adaptation, and international performance. For instance, in their 2015 Fall/Winter issue, *Borrowers and Lenders* published articles such as Giselle Rampaul's "Shakespeare, Empire, and the Trinidad Calypso," Delia Ungureanu's "Translating Autobiography into Fiction: Chiasmus and the Play of the Authorial Mind in *Hamlet* and *Pale Fire*," and Rosa M. Garcia-Periago's "English Shakespeares in Indian Cinema: *36 Chowringhee Lane* and *The Last Lear*."[25] These articles show a range of approaches to global Shakespeare, both with their regional focus (Trinidad, Russia, and India) and methodological approaches (music history, comparative literature, and film studies). Adaptation studies have been a longstanding mainstay of Global Shakespeare; *Borrowers and Lenders* publishes some of the most interesting and provocative adaptation studies in the field.

One challenge facing all journals (regional or global) is making their online content findable by scholars, not only to read, but crucially, to cite. Citation entails a range of intellectual and economic benefits—aiding the circulation of new knowledge in the field and increasing a scholar's opportunities for collaboration and professional promotion. Scholars from the Global South are cited less often: enhancing access to and citation of scholarship by researchers of the Global South, therefore, is necessary to remedy longstanding disparities within the field.

Simply putting a journal online, however, does not make it more findable or cited, particularly when it comes to popular search topics like Shakespeare and *Hamlet*. The challenge of finding and engaging with research on Shakespeare is compounded by the fact that it does not feature only in journals devoted entirely to the study of Shakespeare: it also regularly appears in journals about literature, history, theatre, and beyond. Articles on Shakespeare also occasionally pop up in less-expected places, such as journals about graphic novels or medicine.

---

[25] Desmet and Iyengar, eds. *Borrowers and Lenders*.

Non-Shakespearean journals, too, can be limited to regional circulation or circulation within a particular language group. Sometimes these articles are less likely to be read and cited by Shakespearean scholars, who already have a long list of Shakespeare and early modern studies journals with which to keep up: *Shakespeare Quarterly*, *Shakespeare Bulletin*, *Shakespeare Survey*, *English Literary Renaissance*...the list goes on. It is no wonder, then, that content published in *The Lancet* and *Current Archaeology* (both of which include multiple articles about Shakespeare), as well as other journals from non-literary fields can be overlooked by Shakespeareans. Scholars in the Global North might also overlook Shakespeare journals from outside their region. The *Indian Journal of English Studies* has been publishing for over 60 years, a history comparable to *Shakespeare Quarterly*, but despite its longevity, the journal is less-cited than *Shakespeare Quarterly*, likely partly due to its scope and geographical affiliation.

As all this suggests, disseminating Global Shakespeares happens across media, around the world: theatrically, digitally, and in print. Exhibitions and performances spark essays-in-verse and journal articles, which themselves become the subject of other essays, such as this one. The widespread publication of articles about Shakespeare in journals with broader purviews around the globe is precisely why bibliographies and other aggregators exist: so scholars can locate materials even (especially!) when it appears in publications that are not on their radar. The foundational and important role of enumerative bibliography in Shakespeare studies, as in other fields, is to make materials findable by researchers. Finding materials is often the first step to access.

Digital Projects, Bibliographies, and Databases: Global Shakespeares in the Digital Age

Digital projects are at the vanguard of disseminating Global Shakespeare, where the dynamism of the digital enables multilingual, multimedia options that render material accessible to a wide global audience. In the *Asian Shakespeare Intercultural Archive* (A|S|I|A), users can search in English, Mandarin, Japanese, and Korean across the site's video recordings of Shakespeare productions in Asia, accompanied by the original script and translations in a text window. The *Taiwan Shakespeare Database*, founded by Bi-qi Beatrice Lei, is an open-access online database of Shakespearean productions in Taiwan, offering streamed videos of performance and information about performances, interviews, reviews, and more, in Cantonese, Mandarin, Minnan, Henan dialect, and English. Performances are a pillar of Shakespeare scholarship, and the foundation of theatre history, performance studies, and film studies, among others. Providing access to information about performances beyond theatres in the Global North (especially the United Kingdom and North America), in multiple languages, ensures Shakespeare performers and other production personnel from around the world can become a part of Global Shakespeare studies.

Like digital projects, specialized bibliographies—those that focus on the study of Shakespeare in a given region—play an important role in making global scholarship findable. In the first issue of *Shakespeare in Southern Africa*, the Department of Librarianship at Rhodes University (South Africa) provided "A Shakespeare bibliography of periodical publications in South Africa in 1985 and 1986"; this bibliography continued for decades. Another such list created around the same time, by Rosa Maria Martínez Ascaso, catalogued the articles on Shakespeare held in the Biblioteca de Catalunya in Barcelona: rather than listing the publications that appeared in a particular region, instead, it let scholars know about the Shakespearean articles they could access if they visited a given location.[26] Other notable regional bibliographies include Takashi Sasaki's annual *Shakespeare News from Japan* and monograph *A Bibliography of Shakespeare Studies in Japan (Heisei Period)* as well as Ángel-Luis Pujante and Juan F. Cerdá's *Shakespeare in Spain: An Annotated Bilingual Bibliography*.[27] Local or national bibliographies highlight the importance of Shakespeare reception and scholarship in a given region, which promotes this important scholarship and can make it findable and accessible to a global audience. When these bibliographies are available online, they disseminate their work even more widely.[28]

[26] Martínez Ascaso, "Diàriament, periòdica, sempre Shakespeare."

[27] Sasaki, ed., *Shakespeare News from Japan* (annual); Sasaki, *Nihon Sheikusupia Kenkyusha Shosi*; Pujante and Cerdá, *Shakespeare en España*.

[28] For instance, the bibliographies provided in the journal *Shakespeare in Southern Africa* are available open access from *Sabinet: African Journals*, https://journals.co.za/journal/iseasosa. Digitizing regional bibliographies could be a valuable first step to making the works recorded therein findable.

Other finding aids can take narrower focuses such as Bernice W. Kliman's *Hamletworks*, which focuses entirely on *Hamlet*. *Hamletworks* publishes original scholarly articles, with an entire section of the site devoted to "Global Hamlet,"[29] reprinting essays such as Ruri Li's "Hamlet in China: Translation, Interpretation, and Performance." *Hamletworks* offers features beyond journal articles, including a *Hamlet* Concordance of multiple early texts and digitizations of full-text books such as *Shakespeare: Rare Print Collection* (1900). One of the site's most valuable contributions is that it has digitized the entire print run of *Hamlet Studies*, a journal that ran from 1979 to 2003. *Hamletworks* is both an open-access publisher and an archive: it centralizes a number of resources about *Hamlet* and helps make previously published print-only articles findable and accessible online.

Contrasting regional bibliographies and specialist finding aids, the *World Shakespeare Bibliography* (*WSB*), the premier bibliography of Shakespeare studies, takes a global approach to Shakespeare studies. The *WSB* offers annotations of articles, books, dissertations, professional productions, and digital projects about Shakespeare from 1960–present (as well as listing reviews for these). Despite its broad coverage, the existence of the *WSB* does not negate the need for regionally focused bibliographies, though they will, of course, overlap. Specialized bibliographies often have different coverage from pan-Global ones. Pujante and Cerdá's, for instance, extends back to 1764—almost two hundred years more than the *WSB*, whose ambit begins in 1960. Specialist bibliographies might cover Master's theses, university productions, or newspaper articles, which are not included in the *WSB*.[30] Most importantly, these regional bibliographies show the longstanding importance of global Shakespeare studies by focusing on the local. While a scholar can do a language-limited search in the *WSB*, we do not yet have the functionality of searching by publication place; we cannot differentiate Portuguese publications and productions in Brazil from those in, say, Portugal, the Azores, or Mozambique. Regional bibliographies are needed to open up further (local) research in global Shakespeare studies.

---

[29] Kliman, "Global *Hamlet* Essays" and "Global *Hamlet* Videos" in *Hamletworks*.

[30] For a detailed description of the scope of the *WSB*'s coverage, see http://shakesbib. org/scope.

The *WSB*, however, plays an important role in making global Shakespeare scholarship findable. Scholars who use the *WSB* can choose to limit their search by language, selecting one or more languages. Language-limited searches allow comparatists to find translations and adaptations, while also enabling broader, quantitative analysis. A language-limited search could be used to find scholarship, translations, or performances in a particular language on Shakespeare. Although it indexes and annotates materials in all languages (including, for instance, translations of Shakespeare into Mauritian Creole and Bikol, an indigenous language of the Philippines[31]), the interface of *WSB* is currently only in English. *WSB* offers a brief English-language annotation for the material it covers, while also noting the presence of abstracts in other languages in its source material.

Online journals seek to make their material available by making it findable *and* accessible. Many online journal articles can be found through simple Google searches or through more specialized searches in Google scholar.[32] More and more Shakespeareans are choosing to publish in open-access venues; others are choosing to self-archive their work to make it findable, accessible, and to prevent digital loss. Shakespeareans looking to self-archive their journal articles (in order to preserve and promote their work) can choose to deposit their published materials in an institutional repository or Humanities Commons CORE (Commons Open Repository Exchange).[33] Humanities Commons offers scholars the ability to tag their work with appropriate subjects, such as "Shakespeare" and "LLC Shakespeare" (related to the Languages, Literatures, and Cultures Shakespeare group from the Modern Language Association). The *WSB* also aggregates performances (theatrical, cinematic, and digital, the latter increasingly important following the COVID-19 pandemic), along with scholarship, something that traditional bibliographies do not include as a matter of course.

Because a distinguishing feature of the categories of "Global North" and "Global South" is economic development, money underlies manifold issues of global Shakespeare studies, whether in terms of access

---

[31] Currently, the *WSB* includes two translations in Mauritian Creole and one in Bikol: Etienne, Otelo *an kreol* (*WSB* ad774); Virahsawmy, *Zil Sezar* (*WSB* aaa1794); and Calleja, *Kun Saná si Shakes Taga Sató* (*WSB* aaai1227).

[32] Google Scholar, https://scholar.google.com/.

[33] CORE, https://hcommons.org/core/.

to journals, personal and institutional costs of journal subscriptions, memberships, and access to bibliographies. Even for the high-quality, peer-reviewed, open-access publications discussed (such as *Borrowers and Lenders, Shakespeare Seminar Online,* or *The Journal for Early Modern Studies*) there are costs associated with online publication and maintenance, which can be paid by universities, societies, or presses. Some specialist bibliographies such as the *MLAIB* and the *WSB* are paywalled and available only to those who have a personal subscription or access through their library. One way the *World Shakespeare Bibliography* works to limit the gap in access is by offering free access to the *WSB* and *Shakespeare Quarterly* to the international correspondents who report on local Shakespeare study and performance.[34] Scholars who contribute to the *WSB*, then, are not only credited for their contributions on the site, but also reap the benefits of accessing both the database and one of the flagship journals in the field. Furthermore, the *WSB* links directly to open-access journal articles from their *WSB* entry, which can help scholars without robust institutional subscriptions find full-text resources where possible.

The goal of enumerative bibliographies is to make scholarship findable; as such, the future of bibliography is digital. In Shakespeare studies, the future of enumerative bibliography will need to look to smaller, specialized bibliographies as well as to large projects such as the *WSB*. When it comes to looking at regional scholarship, local experts are pivotal. Curated reading lists by specialists can also play a role in making scholarship findable. Shakespeare studies is a broad field that spans multiple disciplines and includes many different specialities: as Shakespeareans, we need bibliographies that include a diversity of voices and items so that we can better research, that is, listen and learn.

* * *

[34] International correspondents are credited here: http://www.worldshakesbib.org/international-committee-correspondents. For more on the importance of our team of international correspondents, see Estill, "Digital Bibliography and Global Shakespeare." If you are interested in becoming an international correspondent, please contact http://wsb@tamu.edu. Individuals who want to subscribe but do not want to contribute can also do so at a low annual rate (currently $88USD), which is discounted by 15% if they subscribe to either *Shakespeare Quarterly* or *Shakespeare Bulletin*, and discounted by 30% if they subscribe to all three.

With the advent of the digital era, Global Shakespeare studies became more than the study of Shakespeare's impact around the world. Global Shakespeares now include the international publication of works by and about Shakespeare as well as the study of that publication, as this chapter demonstrates. Digital publication and aggregation play a key role in publishing and disseminating scholarship and performance from the Global South, from scholars, and artists who have been historically underrepresented. To carry out research that accounts for the breadth and depth of Shakespeare studies across the world, scholars must move beyond publications from their own areas, regions, countries, continents, and hemispheres, to find emerging perspectives in new venues and locales they might have previously overlooked. This means reconsidering the nature of our discipline, decentring the traditional geographical loci of our field, and looking towards new approaches to Shakespeare and embracing global voices. Digital publication, to varying degrees and in multiple forms, plays a crucial role in the creation and perpetuation of Shakespeare studies in the Global South. The turn to digital informs not just how we publish our journal articles, nor simply the kind of evidence we have and on which we base our claims, but also expands the space and population of the field of Shakespeare studies.

WORKS CITED

"A Shakespeare Bibliography of Periodical Publications in South Africa in 1985 and 1986," *Shakespeare in Southern Africa* 1 (1987): 85–87.

Asian Shakespeare Intercultural Archive (A|S|I|A). Directed by Yong Li Lan. http://a-s-i-a-web.org/en/home.php.

Calleja, G. B. *Kun Saná si Shakes Taga Sa.tó: Su 154 na Kag-Apat ni William Shakespeare*. Naga: Ateneo de Naga University Press, 2017.

CORE. https://hcommons.org/core/.

Craig, Heidi. *World Shakespeare Bibliography*. Oxford: Oxford University Press. www.worldshakesbib.org.

Demeter, Márton. *Academic Knowledge Production and the Global South: Questioning Inequality and Representation*. Cham: Palgrave MacMillan, 2020.

Desmet, Christy and Sujata Iyengar, eds. *Borrowers and Lenders: A Journal of Shakespeare and Appropriation* 9.2 (2015). http://openjournals.libs.uga.edu/borrowers/issue/view/224.

Desmet, Christy, Sujata Iyengar, and Miriam Jacobson, eds. *The Routledge Handbook of Shakespeare and Global Appropriation*. Basingstoke: Routledge, 2020.

Donaldson, Peter S. ed., *Global Shakespeares*. https://globalshakespeares.mit.edu/.

Eng, Ooi Boo "For 'The Age of Shakespeare' Exhibition," *Southeast Asian Review of English*, 2, no. 1, (1981): 63–65. https://ejournal.um.edu.my/index.php/SARE/issue/view/209/AUG1981.

Estill, Laura. "Digital Bibliography and Global Shakespeare," *Scholarly and Research Communication* 5, no. 4 (2014). https://src-online.ca/index.php/src/article/view/187.

Etienne, Richard. *Otelo an kreol*. Port Louis, Mauritius: LPT Editions, 1991.

Gil, Alex. "Through the Breaking-Glass: Spectres of Late-Stage Digital Humanities." Spectrums of DH [digital humanities] lecture, McGill University, 22 April 2021. https://facebook.com/watch/?v=5405976869473681.

Google Scholar. https://scholar.google.com.

Joubin, Alexa Alice. "Global Shakespeares as Methodology," *Shakespeare* 9, no. 3 (2013): 273–90.

Joubin, Alexa Alice. "Global Shakespeares: A Critical Introduction." In *The Palgrave Encyclopedia of Global Shakespeare*, ed. Joubin, Ema Vyroubalova, and Elizabeth Pentland. New York: Palgrave Macmillan, 2021. https://doi.org/10.1007/978-3-319-99378-2_1-1.

Joubin, Alexa Alice, Ema Vyroubalova, and Elizabeth Pentland, eds. *The Palgrave Encyclopedia of Global Shakespeare*. New York: Palgrave Macmillan, 2021. https://doi.org/10.1007/978-3-319-99378-2

KL Shakespeare. http://www.klshakespeare.com.my/about-us.

Kliman, Bernice W. et al. *Hamletworks*. http://hamletworks.org.

Kok, Su Mei. "'What's Past is Prologue': Postcolonialism, Globalisation, and the Demystification of Shakespeare in Malaysia," *Southeast Asian Review of English* 54, no. 1 (2017). https://doi.org/10.22452/sare.vol54no1.4.

Kujawińska Courtney, Krystyna, and John M. Mercer, eds. *Globalization of Shakespeare in the Nineteenth Century*. Lewiston: Edwin Mellen, 2003.

Lei, Bi-Qi Beatrice. "Digital Representations of Contemporary Shakespeare Performances." *Early Modern Digital Review*. https://emdr.itercommunity.org, forthcoming.

Li, Ruri. "*Hamlet* in China: Translation, Interpretation and Performance." *Global Shakespeares*, ed. Peter S. Donaldson. https://globalshakespeares.mit.edu/extra/hamlet-in-china-translation-interpretation-and-performance/; Reprinted on *HamletWorks* ed. Bernice W. Kliman.

Martínez Ascaso, Rosa Maria. "Diàriament, periòdica, sempre Shakespeare: Crítiques, comentaris i interpretacions sobre Shakespeare i les seves obres, a les revistes i diaris del fons de la 'Biblioteca de Catalunya' de Barcelona," *Cuadernos de Traducción y Interpretación* 5–6 (1985): 137–51.

Multicultural Shakespeare: Translation, Appropriation and Performance. Edited by Kawachi Yoshiko and Krystyna Kujawińska Courtney. https://czasopisma. uni.lodz.pl/szekspir/about.

New, W. H. "A Guide to Canadian Fiction," *Southeast Asian Review of English* 3, no. 1 (1981): 1–8. https://sare.um.edu.my/index.php/SARE/issue/vie w/210.

Pujante, Ángel-Luis, and Juan F. Cerdá, *Shakespeare en España: Bibliografía anotada bilingüe. Shakespeare in Spain: An Annotated Bilingual Bibliography.* Murcia: Universidad de Murcia and Universidad de Granada, 2015.

Roy, Amitava et al. Theatre International: East-West Persprctives on Theatre. Vol. 1.1 (1994). https://www.ssei.org.in/TI/VOL%20I.pdf.

Sasaki, Takashi. *Nihon Sheikusupia Kenkyusha Shosi (Heisei-hen) [A Bibliography of Shakespeare Studies in Japan (Heisei Period)].* Tochigi: Econ, 2009.

Sasaki, Takashi, ed. *Shakespeare News from Japan.* Tokyo: Komazawa University Shakespeare Institute, annual.

Shakespeare in Southern Africa. https://ajol.info/index.php/sisa.

Skupin, Michael. "Shakespeare Comes to Indonesia," *Multicultural Shakespeare: Translation, Appropriation and Performance* 10, no. 25 (2013): 99–119. https://doi.org/10.2478/mstap-2013-0008.

Sumardjo, Trisno. *Hamlet, Pangeran Denmark.* Jakarta: Jajasan Pembangunan, 1950.

———. *Saudagar Venezia.* Tr. Trisno Sumardjo Jakarta: Balai Pustaka, 1950.

Taiwan Shakespeare Database. Directed by Bi-qi Beatrice Lei. http://shakes peare.digital.ntu.edu.tw/shakespeare/home.php?Language=en.

Virahsawmy, Dev. *Zil Sezar.* Port Louis, Mauritius, 1999.

CHAPTER 3

From 'English Never Loved Us' to JAM at the Windybrow: Covid-Era Digital Shakespeares in/from South Africa

Chris Thurman

Abstract This essay considers the ways in which various digital initiatives and campaigns employed Shakespeare in South Africa as Covid-19 took its toll on the country. In some cases, Shakespearean invocations, allusions and appropriations were opportunistic and incidental: from the Pendoring advertising awards' 'English Never Loved Us' campaign to a curious citation from Julius Caesar in defence of corrupt politicians in the African National Congress. In other cases, performer-oriented initiatives like #lockdownshakespeare or the Market Theatre's 'Chilling with the Bard' series promoted a more popular and accessible form of Shakespeare. The overall result was a circulation of bitesize Shakespeare—a fragmentation that may have lacked coherence but provided a valuable counterpoint to the 'worthy', weighty Shakespeare that most South Africans associate primarily with educational curricula.

C. Thurman (✉)
University of the Witwatersrand, Johannesburg, South Africa
e-mail: christopher.thurman@wits.ac.za

A. Sen (ed.), *Digital Shakespeares from the Global South*, Global Shakespeares, https://doi.org/10.1007/978-3-031-04787-9_3

37

Keywords Lockdownshakespeare · Bitesize Shakespeare and South Africa · Coronavirus pandemic

INTRODUCTION: RECALLING BC
(BEFORE COVIDIGITALIZATION)

In 2019, I wrote an article about digital Shakespeares and education in South Africa for a special issue of *Research in Drama Education* on 'Teaching Shakespeare: Digital Processes'.[1] Surveying the limited Shakespearean digital resources produced in South Africa to support educators and learners—but also, by implication, decrying the limited digital content made for arts audiences outside of a specifically educational context—that article ended by presenting something of a manifesto for the work of *Shakespeare ZA* (https://shakespeare.org.za), a website I had founded under the auspices of the Shakespeare Society of Southern Africa in 2017. In short, the aim was to expand and accelerate the modest success that *Shakespeare ZA* had achieved in commissioning and producing digital Shakespearean content by and for South Africans: teaching resources, digitized versions of books long since out of print and above all audio and video material aplenty. The article was published in January 2020. It hardly needs explaining why the manifesto was soon out of date. With Covid-19 putting in-person performance indefinitely on hold, and having a similar effect on in-person teaching, South African Shakespeares followed the global pattern and went virtual. The amount of digitally distributed and consumed material related to Shakespeare in a South African context would increase almost exponentially over the next eighteen months. Call it Covidigitalization.

Of course, other aspects of digital and/or Shakespearean production and consumption that I outlined in that article were not so readily rendered out of date. An appreciation of South Africa's "digital divide", which tends to follow the economic, social and geographical divisions produced by colonialism and apartheid, remains a necessary component to any analysis of digital Shakespeares in and from the country. While

---

[1] Thurman, 'Shakespeare.za: Digital Shakespeares and education in South Africa', 49–67.

Covid has no doubt increased access to virtual content for many South Africans, material constraints persist. Another factor discussed in my article that has not been fundamentally altered by Covid is Shakespeare's position in South Africa—both in the education landscape and in the arts sector. Shakespeare remains associated with Britishness/Englishness, with elitism and aspirationalism, with the tedium of the textbook rather than the provocation of performance. One factor, however, has changed since the early months of 2020: the sharp increase in digital content produced in South Africa has given performing artists and other "content creators" (to use a bland descriptor) access to global audiences in a way that few of them would previously have dared to seek, even if the technology and the platforms were already available.

Having started this essay with a reference to my own scholarly and public-facing work, there is a risk that I will continue in a somewhat solipsistic vein, describing South African digital Shakespeares only in terms of those projects in which I have been involved. I will attempt to avoid falling into that trap; nevertheless, it should be noted here that Shakespeare ZA and the Tsikinya-Chaka Centre (TCC), a research unit I established at Wits University, are committed to supporting and promoting the work of digital Shakespeares in South Africa. There is a sense, then, in which it is not entirely inappropriate to follow the halting manifesto of my earlier article with a critical self-appraisal or a report on work-in-progress. It is my hope that doing so provides an opportunity for further reflection on the paradigm of 'Digital Shakespeares from the Global South' as applied to South Africa.

Bitesize Shakespeares

How do we define "digital Shakespeares in/from South Africa" as a category? I would suggest that, for a proper survey of the terrain, it should be understood in the most capacious terms possible. This could stretch to include Shakespearean invocations, allusions and appropriations that are opportunistic and incidental. I am not undertaking a survey, so two examples must suffice here, but they speak powerfully to the political and historical dimensions of Shakespeare in South Africa.

In July 2020, the annual Pendoring Advertising Awards, which recognize innovation and creativity in marketing in South African languages, launched with the theme 'English Never Loved Us' (a common joke among multilingual South Africans who speak English as an additional language). The primary figure invoked in this campaign—the pre-eminent symbol of Englishness—was Shakespeare. Short videos, memes and other materials shared widely via social media set Shakespeare in opposition to South African languages like isiZulu, Setswana, Tshivenda and Afrikaans, asking:

> Oh Lomeo, Lomeo, wherefore art thou my isiZulu Lomeo?
> "To be or not to be" in Setswana. That is the real question, William.
> What is iambic pentameter in Tshivenda?
> "To be or not to be" in Afrikaans. Dis die ware vraag, ou Willie.[2]

There are a few levels of irony here, and it is uncertain how many of these the Pendoring team had in mind. Certainly, few South Africans know about the history of translating Shakespeare into some of the languages casually cited here (and another four or five official languages besides these), or about current practice by theatre-makers, scholars and language activists seeking to build on that tradition.

The joke on the pronunciation of 'Romeo' with an 'L' is half at Shakespeare's expense and half at the expense of isiZulu speakers; its comic edge is blunted somewhat by the fact that an isiZulu version of the play by Sabatha Ngcobo, *uLomeyo noJula*, was performed by a group of students at the Durban University of Technology in 2019 and is currently being revised and edited for publication by a team working under the auspices of the TCC. That is hardly public knowledge, but it would be somewhat disappointing if those behind the Pendoring Awards, pushing a brand that trades on advocacy for South African languages, did not have at least a passing familiarity with the life and work of Solomon T. Plaatje: journalist, linguist, historian, novelist and founder member of the South African Native National Congress (later the ANC). As part of his mission to protect and enhance the cultural and linguistic heritage of the Batswana, Plaatje translated a handful of Shakespeare's plays into Setswana. These did not include *Hamlet*, but two of them (*Diphosho-phosho* [*The Comedy of Errors*] in 1930 and *Dintshontsho tsa bo-Juliuse Kesara* [*Julius Caesar*] in 1937) are generally considered the first published translations of Shakespeare into any African language. If one was inclined to be even more pedantic, one could point out not only that there are at least three translations of *Hamlet* into Afrikaans,

---

but that the history of translating Shakespeare into Afrikaans attests to that language's political and economic power in the second half of the twentieth century (and to a persisting linguistic power imbalance that is, incidentally, reflected in the fact that 'Dis die ware vraag, ou Willie' ['That's the real question, Old Will'] does not get an equivalent Setswana rendering). And, yes, all of these translations form part of a Shakespeare ZA/TCC digitization project; and, yes, they will soon be accessible via the digital Sol Plaatje Archive of Shakespeare in African Languages; and, yes, I am overly invested in all of this, and I should learn to take a joke.

On to more weighty matters, then. In the same month that the Pendoring 'English Never Loved Us' campaign was launched, the ANC in Limpopo decided to reinstate provincial treasurer Danny Msiza and deputy chairperson Florence Radzilani despite the pair's implication in fraudulent activities—specifically, in the VBS Mutual Bank scandal, which entailed the theft of over two billion rands from customer savings. Again, an irony-laden Shakespearean citation came to the fore; in this case, an amateurish bit of dodgy digital design that did the rounds on Facebook, Twitter and WhatsApp (mis)quoting *Julius Ceasar* [sic]: 'Cowards die many times before their actual death. The valiant never tastes death but once' (Fig. 3.1).

Again, it is impossible to tell if the propagandist behind this message was invoking the authority of Nelson Mandela, who famously signed his name alongside the same passage in the Robben Island "Bible"— a copy of the *Collected Works* circulated among political prisoners who had been incarcerated by the apartheid regime.[3] It may be that s/he was simply continuing a venerable South African political tradition of quoting Shakespeare out of context.[4] Either way, the decline of the ANC from a liberation movement to a mechanism for shameless racketeering is writ large in this Shakespearean fragment.

I have discussed these examples because they attest to the role that (digital) Shakespeare tends to play in South Africa's (digital) public discourse: he/it is a symbol or a shorthand point of reference, rather than a body of work meriting any sustained attention. 2020 also, however, saw

---

[3] See Schalkwyk, *Hamlet's Dreams: The Robben Island Shakespeare* and Desai, *Reading Revolution: Shakespeare on Robben Island*.

[4] See Hofmeyr, 'Reading Debating / Debating Reading: The case of the Lovedale Debating Society, or Why Mandela quotes Shakespeare', 258–77 and Roux, 'Shakespeare and Tragedy in South Africa: From *Black Hamlet* to *A Dream Deferred*', 1–14.

Fig. 3.1 Welcome back home cadres (*Source* Twitter)

two initiatives that sought to intervene in and disrupt the assumptions that South Africans have about what Shakespeare "means", or for that matter what Shakespeare looks and sounds like. These were performer-oriented projects insofar as they provided platforms to promote the talents of individual actors while the country's stages were dark, but they also aimed to produce a more popular and accessible form of Shakespeare for a wider South African audience—an audience that, in 2020, had an increased appetite for digital content and was spending even more time on social media.

Firstly, there was Shakespeare ZA's #lockdownshakespeare campaign, which encouraged actors stuck at home to film themselves delivering a monologue (entrants received a modest R1000 payment for participating). The result was a library of some fifty videos, first posted on social media, then loaded to the #lockdownshakespeare YouTube channel and embedded on Shakespeare ZA. Initially envisaged as a digital resource for South African educators, students and theatre makers, #lockdownshakespeare caught the attention of scholars and teachers in other countries. In a review for *Shakespeare Bulletin*, Henry Bell of the University of the West of Scotland writes:

> As a lecturer in performance studies, like many of my colleagues across the education sector, I have had to adapt teaching materials and assessments away from the live event of theater and venture into the world of self-taping. Both the technical and creative choices of the films contained with the #lockdownshakespeare project have provided a fantastic resource for me to use as a teacher to give examples of how the restrictions implemented through the various COVID-19 lockdown rules around the world can be a stimulus for creative practice.
>
> ...
>
> In a time of uncertainty surrounding the future of professional performing arts practice, it has been a source of inspiration to stumble across this excellent work through the global connectivity of the internet. Perhaps #lockdownshakespeare could serve as a lesson to theatre companies around the world as an example of how to both support and promote artists, whilst concurrently creating a first-rate cultural product that is accessible to anybody with an internet connection.[5]

Then came the Market Theatre's 'Chilling with the Bard' season, which saw ten South African actresses taking to the stage of an empty John Kani Theatre and performing monologues for the camera. Three others recorded themselves off-site, but for Market Artistic Director James Ngcobo it was important to film as much as possible in the physical space of the theatre to remind audiences that 'we might be closed but stories are never on pause'.[6]

---

[5] Bell, '*#lockdownshakespeare* (review)', 526–7.

[6] James Ngcobo in The Market Theatre ZA, 'Market Theatre Chilling with the Bard Season Promo with James Ngcobo' (video). Online: https://www.youtube.com/watch?v=nyRWP1W4p1w.

Timed to coincide with Women's Month in South Africa, 'Chilling with the Bard' was launched in August, and was presented as a two-pronged form of activism—represented in the hashtags generated by the Market when promoting the videos. On the one hand, this was a project undertaken in solidarity with theatre-makers around the country whose livelihoods were at risk: hence the affirmation that #TheatreWillRiseAgain. On the other hand, it was a contribution to public discourse in and about Women's Month (a source of much contestation in South Africa, where gender-based violence is recognized as another "epidemic" but where politicians' platitudes about addressing this scourge have little to no effect) because women were performing parts traditionally seen as "for men": hence the provocation of #ShakeHerSpear.

Although the 'Chilling with the Bard' season sought to be subversive, the contradiction one might read into its title—the hierarchical and high-art baggage that comes with invoking 'the Bard' arguably precludes the low-key, easygoing egalitarianism of 'chilling'—extended into the packaging and promotion of the videos, which reinforced very staid, conventional and even conservative (Anglocentric, Bardolatrous) notions about Shakespeare in performance. The emphasis on South African performers, an 'amazing combination of talent that will breathe new life to these 400 years old works' [sic], became less pronounced as the messaging lapsed into tedious Shakespearean universality: each speech, viewers were told, carries 'a theme that has some pertinence with what is going on around us … that is the joy of Shakespeare, his works remain timeless and relevant. When we read and watch one of Shakespeare classic plays [sic], we gain a deeper understating of the world around us'.[7] In a puff piece tellingly titled 'Shakespeare is the Man For All Seasons with Women Breaking the Acting Mould', Diane de Beer quotes Ngcobo effervescing about the Bard: 'It is really a marvel that almost 400 years after he wrote this great literature, we are still intrigued and engulfed in this magnificent work of brilliance. Shakespeare poured his heart and imagination into these wondrous stories that have been acclaimed, enjoyed, and staged over the years'.[8]

---

[7] The Market Theatre ZA, 'Market Theatre William Shakespeare Sonnet 13 & *Twelfth Night* by Renate Stuurman and Leila Henriques' (text accompanying video). Online: https://www.youtube.com/watch?v=RO7qKLFV72I.

[8] Ngcobo in Diane de Beer, 'Shakespeare is the Man For All Seasons with Women Breaking the Acting Mould', *De Beer Necessities*, 18 August

The videos themselves are introduced by a graphic sequence that features a rotating ruff and a set of red velvet curtains being drawn across an imagined proscenium stage—a strangely anachronistic bit of iconography, especially odd given that it has nothing in common with the Market Theatre's actual performance spaces. For the videos recorded on the John Kani (thrust) stage, each actress stepped onto a raised platform visible in the shot, with back-lighting and smoke creating an explicitly theatrical setting and style. This may be contrasted with the self-filmed #lockdownshakespeare videos, for which performers tended to adopt a more cinematographic approach to location (mostly out of necessity). I will return to the question of digital Shakespeares that have their origins on stage, as opposed to those that are more site-specific, later in this essay.

In the early months of South Africans' experience of Covid lockdowns and constraints, resource limitations and a slightly panicked sense of "scrambling"—wanting to continue making work but also having to make things up along the way, under new, adverse and untested circumstances—prevented performers and directors from producing full digital or filmic versions of the plays. The overall result of this, compounded by the kinds of popular appropriations of or borrowings from Shakespeareans that I mentioned earlier, was a circulation of bitesize Shakespeares: a fragmentation that may have lacked coherence but that (notwithstanding the occasional ruff or velvet curtains) provided a valuable counterpoint to the "worthy", weighty Shakespeare that most South Africans associate primarily with school English curricula and with vestiges of British colonialism. While Covid-19 decimated the country's performing arts sector, in the case of Shakespeare it nonetheless created a window of opportunity to disrupt a cliché set of expectations.

From Fragmentation to Curation

At this point, we may return to the problem of definition. What can be considered "digital Shakespeares"? Is anything Shakespearean on YouTube a form of digital Shakespeare? In a South African context, can anything published or promoted on Shakespeare ZA—a Padlet or Spark Page shared by a teacher, a searchable PDF of an out-of-print translation, an embedded video—be described as a digital resource? The answer

2020. Online: https://debeernecessities.com/2020/08/18/shakespeare-is-the-man-for-all-seasons-with-women-breaking-the-acting-mould/.

must be yes. Still, some disaggregation is required. Recall for instance the global early-Covid phenomenon of making recordings of past stage productions more widely (mostly temporarily) available: NT Live, Shakespeare's Globe and the Royal Shakespeare Company released previously restricted content, while platforms like Marquee TV sought to transport the stage into the living room. This was an opportunity, too, for South African Shakespeares that first had their life on stage—and had made little to no imprint on the local arts scene—to be introduced, or re-introduced and newly promoted, on screen: the collaborative and experimental work *Umsebenzi ka Bra Shakes* [Working with Bro Shakes] (filmed at the Centre for the Less Good Idea in 2019) was on Vimeo, Greg Homann's concept treatment for a production of *Twelfth Night* (filmed at the Ramolao Makhene Theatre in 2019) was loaded to YouTube and Brett Bailey's version of Verdi's *Macbeth* with Third World Bunfight (filmed at the Teatro Politeama in Naples in 2014) took pride of place on the programme of the fully virtual National Arts Festival.

Having this material online made for a modest and somewhat messy archive, a rabbit-hole for eager South African Shakespeareans—performers and audiences missing the theatre, or perhaps even teachers and students momentarily unshackled from the iron ball of the curriculum—to explore, containing meals more substantial than the bitesize monologues. It was only in 2021, however, as we collectively and reluctantly accepted that the implications of Covid would still dominate life for another year at least, that a more sustained curatorial and cohesive approach to digital Shakespeares would become evident. For scholars, this meant taking stock of the pivot online, mapping out the digital scene and drawing transnational connections in doing so. For instance, #lockdownshakespeare was the subject of a virtual seminar in which the South African experiment was linked to Bell's use of self-filming as both a pedagogical and a performative tool for his students in Scotland; in turn, this practice was compared to the work of Ghanaian theatre company Act for Change, whose recordings of scenes performed at historically significant locations in Jamestown (in Accra) suggested new possibilities for site-specific filming as a means of engaging with Shakespeare and/as colonial history.[9]

---

[9] See 'Lockdown Shakespeares: Transnational Explorations', a seminar co-hosted by the Creative Media Academy (University of the West of Scotland) and the Tsikinya-Chaka Centre (University of the Witwatersrand), 31 March 2021. A recording of the seminar,

For theatre-makers turned film-makers, curating digital Shakespeares—on a small budget—meant finding more appealing ways to use Zoom-type platforms, creating work for the screen that was neither theatrical nor filmic but a hybrid of the two and, moreover, that overcame the difficulty of audience members' excessive familiarity with the generic "virtual meeting" format. One South African example stands out here: a 'live-online reading' of *Hamlet* directed by Neil Coppen (with associate directors Buhle Ngaba and Bianca Amato).[10] Marguerite de Waal provides some useful background and an account of the liminal status of this "production":

> Originally slated for performance in June 2020 at The Fugard Theatre in Cape Town, Coppen's *Hamlet* was well-positioned to become a seminal new production of Shakespeare in South Africa ... In early 2021, a year after the start of the pandemic, The Fugard announced that it was closing its doors permanently. The theatre was thus survived by the online reading of *Hamlet*, one of the last projects it helped to nurture. This *Hamlet* was produced on Zoom, hosted on the website of the KKNK (Klein Karoo Nasionale Kunstefees), and made available to audiences for free ... [It] has been described variously in marketing materials as a live, once-off reading, a rehearsed reading, a work in progress. Now, after the live performance, it remains available on the KKNK website as a recording of a once-off reading. It is not a stage production, but it is a work clearly envisioned for the stage. It might, in future, make its way to live performances in a physical theatre: a consummation devoutly to be wished.[11]

Coppen's *Hamlet* benefited from this ambiguity. Amato gave a kind of voice-over narration as she read the stage directions and scene descriptions, so the viewer could imagine a spectacle onstage even as the onscreen aesthetic was minimalist and uniform (black costumes and backdrops). Some moments that would require elaborate effects to execute onstage were achieved through simple devices—clever use of lighting, props and positioning, with the performer leaning into or drawing away

including sample videos from South Africa, Scotland and Ghana, is available at https://www.tsikinya-chaka.org/news-events-and-features/seminar-lockdown-shakespeare.

[10] The reading/production can be viewed at https://www.kknk.co.za/eng/hamlet/ (starts at 24:30).

[11] de Waal, '*Hamlet* 2021's Outrageous Fortune', 54.

from the camera (one thinks in particular of Ngaba's Ophelia drowning, or Wiseman Sithole as Hamlet's father's ghost/the ancestor king).

I hesitate to write too enthusiastically about this virtual *Hamlet* because the Tsikinya-Chaka Centre (TCC) was among the producing partners. It is equally difficult, however, to write about digital Shakespeares in South Africa without discussing the work of the TCC and its partners because "curating" digital Shakespeares is part of the Centre's mandate. It is the driving principle behind the expansion of the translation digitization project from Shakespeare ZA's pilot exhibition into the Sol Plaatje Archive of Shakespeare in African Languages. It is also crucial to the TCC's more public-facing initiatives, such as the podcast series *Shake the Sword!*, which profiles scholars, translators, educators and theatre makers working at the intersection of Shakespeare, transnationalism and multilingualism (the first season focuses on African Shakespeares). And it is the means by which the TCC has been best able to support and promote performing artists in South Africa.

Two such enterprises are worth mentioning here. In April 2021, the Joburg Theatre—under the auspices of its development programme, the Duma Ndlovu Academy—staged a multilingual production of *Macbeth* that had grown out of a workshop process facilitated by Jerry Mntonga, Michael Mazibuko and Sarah Roberts. During this process, the ensemble of young actors, freed from the constraints of being told how to "do Shakespeare", translated words, lines and passages into their home languages and interwove these with the Shakespearean text. The result was an innovative and invigorating production, but after a short run for reduced audiences between South Africa's second and third Covid waves, a planned schools' tour had to be postponed and eventually cancelled. Fortunately, Mntonga had recorded hours of footage: not just rehearsals and performances, but also lengthy cast discussions about Shakespeare, language, race and cultural practices. The TCC was thus able to fund a recuperative project, commissioning the editing of the video material into different packages for use in educational contexts (in lieu of a schools' tour) but also as a contribution to the growing constellation of publically available digital South African Shakespeare content.[12]

The TCC's emphasis on using Shakespeare as a means of promoting South African languages—as languages of teaching and learning, as well

---

[12] At the time of writing, this editing process is still underway.

Fig. 3.2 Filming Lwazi Mayeki as Richard III (JAM at the Windybrow) (*Source* Chris Thurman)

as of creative practice—resulted in a parallel project that was conceived at the outset in filmic rather than theatrical terms. Johannesburg Awakening Minds (JAM) is a theatre company started by Dorothy Ann Gould that is often presented through the rather clumsy shorthand of "homeless Shakespeare"; while everyone currently in the group has indeed lived on the street, and while they have lost members to violence, disease and drugs, the story of JAM is not merely one of indigence. A number of JAM performers have secured professional acting opportunities. Thanks to the commitment of former Market Theatre foundation CEO Ismail Mohamed, the ensemble now has a permanent base at the Windybrow Arts Complex—a restored Randlord building that is an architectural anomaly among the tenement flats of Hillbrow in Johannesburg's inner

Fig. 3.3 Filming T. Kalombo Louis as Mark Antony (JAM at the Windybrow) (*Source* Chris Thurman)

city.[13] In order to pre-empt the condescension that so often comes with the telling of the JAM story or with viewing their work, the TCC teamed up with How Now Brown Cow Productions to showcase the performers not as "charity cases" but as pioneers: they have translated various monologues and sonnets into South African languages (isiXhosa, isiZulu, Siswati) and, performed as if with a knowing wink, their repertoire includes the Mechanicals scenes from *A Midsummer Night's Dream*.

---

[13] Randlords is a collective term for the investors and industrialists who became enormously wealthy from the discovery of diamonds and gold in Kimberley and Johannesburg towards the end of the nineteenth century.

The *Dream* scenes in particular show how the JAM members' individual linguistic and cultural perspectives have forged a translanguaged Shakespeare rarely seen in South Africa, even though translanguaging is an everyday practice for most people living in the country.

Again with the dual aim of producing resources for educators, students and fellow-actors as well as multiple forms of content for the general public—YouTube videos of individual speeches, behind-the-scenes and interview footage intended for circulation on social media, a short film comprising the *Dream* material under the playful title *A Midsummer Ice Cream*, and a documentary-style feature drawing on all of this—the JAM performers were filmed in carefully selected spaces in and around the Windybrow complex (Figs. 3.2 and 3.3).[14] This focus on the Windybrow as location went beyond a reductive feel-good assertion that it is the group's "home"; instead, it underscored a nuanced situatedness, complementing the cross-pollination between Shakespearean text and South African languages while not shying away from the paradoxes of this mutually informing relationship. As it happens, the defunct theatre space that abuts the old Windybrow mansion was, in the 1990s, host to a series of annual productions of *Julius Caesar* (directed by John Matshikiza and Walter Chakela) that constitute a significant albeit largely undocumented facet of Shakespearean performance in the early post-apartheid period—notable for having black directors and predominantly black casts, and for their engagement with a history of translating Shakespeare in South Africa that goes back to Plaatje's *Juliuse Kesara*. The Windybrow buildings have a complicated history spanning over a century. Their position in a part of Johannesburg that some would vindicate as this Afropolitan city's beating heart, but others would damn as a bleak corner of dirt, danger and neglect, speaks to the complexities of a democratic South Africa yet to come to terms with its past. Yet there is also a sense in which the digital documenting of the JAM ensemble's connection to the place—via Shakespeare—gestures towards, if not a utopian future, then at least something approximating hope.

---

[14] The videos of the performances, collected under the titles *JAM AT THE WINDYBROW* and *A Midsummer Ice Cream*, can be viewed here: https://www.tsikinya-chaka.org/news-events-and-features/jam-at-the-windybrow and here: https://www.tsikinya-chaka.org/news-events-and-features/a-midsummer-ice-cream.

Conclusion: Local Sites, Local Languages, Global Digital Shakespeares

As I have already suggested, embracing a wide definition of digital Shakespeares—particularly when it comes to performed Shakespeare, as opposed to textual resources—invites a somewhat deflating question: are there actually any contemporary Shakespearean phenomena that could be altogether excluded from this category? (In which case, does the descriptor have any real value?) It would be a rarity indeed to find a "traditional" staged performance today that is not filmed or digitally documented in some way, and that also has no social media marketing or other forms of digital footprint. So perhaps we cannot simplistically delineate "digital" and "analogue" Shakespeares. But it is interesting to observe how and when the digital enables the non-digital (if we are to use those terms), and vice-versa.

Consider, for example, a moment in the 'Lockdown Shakespeare' online seminar that saw the attendees—who had thus far engaged with site-specific, isolated and self-recorded filmic Shakespeares in semi-locked-down South Africa, Ghana and Scotland—unexpectedly joining an in-person rehearsal, as Fumban Phiri of the Malawian theatre education organization Youth Developmental Collaboration (YDC) walked with his smartphone into a Blantyre venue where a YDC ensemble was workshopping scenes from *Macbeth*.[15] This was a brief insight into idiosyncratic "local" and material staging conditions for a "global" audience spread across a dozen countries.

Of course, such Covid-context hybrids of "digital" and "analogue" modes of theatre practice are only an extension and an expansion of what was already occurring pre-Covid. In any event, "digital versus non-digital" does not equate to "virtual versus in-person" or "screen versus stage". A prominent pre-Covid Shakespearean example (one among many) of the limitations of such binaries is the Royal Shakespeare Company 2016–17 production of *The Tempest*, which used motion capture technology to create an avatar of Ariel incorporated into live performance. Another is the combination of digital technology and traditional stage practice used to great effect in filming stage performances specifically for digital distribution and consumption. In South Africa, this became possible when well-resourced organizations such as the National

---

[15] See 'Lockdown Shakespeares: Transnational Explorations' (from 1:10:30).

Arts Festival built substantial virtual platforms in 2020 and 2021, but there was no "Shakespearean" content created and presented in this way—unless one includes a show such as Buhle Ngaba's *Swan Song*—and certainly nothing that might be seen as equivalent to the 'Viral Shakespeare' lockdown phenomena identified by Pascale Aebischer.[16]

Despite the blurring of the "digital" and the "non-digital" in the archive of recorded Shakespeare productions and events, it is nonetheless important to keep in mind the differences between performances conceived primarily for in-person audiences and those directed at the outset towards video viewers. Coppen's *Hamlet*, as we have seen, is ambiguous on this score. More readily differentiated are the Joburg Theatre *Macbeth* (out of which digital content emerged, although it was driven by in-person theatre performance) and the JAM project at the Windybrow (which was envisaged from the outset as both digital and site-specific). Built into such distinctions are intentions and expectations around audiences; if *Macbeth* was conceived for "local" audiences—not just South African, but in Johannesburg specifically—then JAM at the Windybrow was positioned for a wider audience by dint of its digital/filmic imagination. Yet, as I have suggested, its origins at a particular location—a specific building in a specific part of a specific city—instantiate the claim that what characterizes digital Shakespeares in/from South Africa (and arguably across the Global South) is an insistence that the digital is always sustained in relation to the material. This applies, to some degree, to material constraints on performance practice: limited resources and funding. More significant, however, is materiality understood as historicity. That is to say, digital Shakespeares in/from South Africa cannot be severed from the country's history and its present-day socioeconomic consequences.

Finally, I want to underscore how the digital turn enables multilingual and accessible Shakespeares—not just through practical conventions and tools such as subtitling, closed captions or auto-translation but, more significantly, because it makes possible the breadth of reach that is required to change attitudes. In the #lockdownshakespeare videos, as

·

[16] See Aebischer, *Viral Shakespeare*. *Swan Song* was conceived during Ngaba's residency with the Royal Shakespeare Company in Stratford-upon-Avon, and incorporates elements of *Romeo and Juliet* among other Shakespearean allusions, quotations and echoes; see Thurman, 'Kunene and the Swan: Two Approaches to Biography, History and Shakespeare in South African Theatre', 65–96.

Henry Bell notes, there is a (disappointing) dearth of performers who chose to engage with Shakespeare in a language other than English. This is a reminder of how much work remains to be done in terms of advocacy for South African languages generally and, in particular, making the case that multilingual Shakespeares in the classroom, on the stage and (especially) on the screen can be a means towards this end. The Joburg Theatre *Macbeth*, in a "traditional" theatre space, evinced what I have previously described as the ideal of 'code-switching virtuosity' (more properly, translanguaging): when a multilingual South African ensemble performs Shakespeare for an audience with an equally impressive linguistic repertoire.[17] But this production would have had a negligible impact in terms of changing perceptions about Shakespeare and South Africa's linguistic landscape if it was only shared with a dozen Covid-restricted audiences during a two-week run. Turned into a digital product, however, it can join the JAM Windybrow videos and other TCC projects like the *Shake the Sword!* podcast and the Sol Plaatje Archive in a much-needed "advertising" (or perhaps "conscientising") campaign to change both local and international mindsets about South African languages and Shakespeare, making inroads into the public sphere and the education sector alike.

In 2019, this was something like the declared aim of Shakespeare ZA. In 2020, as the institutional groundwork was laid for what would become the Tsikinya-Chaka Centre, Covidigitalization had a positive impact on digital Shakespeares in/from South Africa. And in 2021, we started taking full advantage of digital media to make multilingual South African Shakespeares more prominent.

WORKS CITED

Aebischer, Pascale. *Viral Shakespeare: Performance in the Time of Pandemic* (Cambridge: Cambridge University Press, 2021).

Bell, Henry. '*#lockdownshakespeare* (review)'. *Shakespeare Bulletin* 38.3 (2020): 526–7.

Coppen, Neil (director). *Hamlet*. A live-online reading presented by DGC, in partnership with VRT and the KKNK, in association with the Tsikinya-Chaka Centre (Wits University) and the Centre for Creative Arts (University of KwaZulu-Natal), 31 May 2021. Online: https://www.kknk.co.za/eng/hamlet/.

---

[17] Thurman, 'Accentism, Anglocentrism, and Multilingualism in South African Shakespeares', 115.

De Beer, Diane. 'Shakespeare is the Man For All Seasons with Women Breaking the Acting Mould'. *De Beer Necessities*, 18 August 2020. Online: https:// debeernecessities.com/2020/08/18/shakespeare-is-the-man-for-all-seasons-with-women-breaking-the-acting-mould/.

Desai, Ashwin. *Reading Revolution: Shakespeare on Robben Island* (Pretoria: Unisa Press, 2012).

De Waal, Marguerite. '*Hamlet* 2021's Outrageous Fortune', *Shakespeare in Southern Africa* 34 (2021): 53–56.

Hofmeyr, Isabel. 'Reading Debating / Debating Reading: The Case of the Lovedale Debating Society, or Why Mandela Quotes Shakespeare', in *Africa's Hidden Histories: Everyday Literacy and Making the Self*, ed. Karin Barber (Bloomington: Indiana University Press, 2006), pp. 258–77.

'Lockdown Shakespeares: Transnational Explorations'. A Seminar Co-hosted by the Creative Media Academy (University of the West of Scotland) and the Tsikinya-Chaka Centre (University of the Witwatersrand), 31 March 2021. Online: https://www.tsikinya-chaka.org/news-events-and-fea tures/seminar-lockdown-shakespeare.

Market Theatre ZA. 'Market Theatre Chilling with the Bard Season Promo with James Ngcobo' (video), 12 August 2020. Online: https://www.youtube. com/watch?v=nyRWP1W4p1w.

Market Theatre ZA. 'Market Theatre William Shakespeare Sonnet 13 & Twelfth Night by Renate Stuurman and Leila Henriques' (video and accompanying text), 17 September 2020. Online: https://www.youtube.com/watch?v=RO7 qKLFV72I.

Pendoring Awards, Facebook. https://www.facebook.com/PendoringAwards.

Roux, Daniel. 'Shakespeare and Tragedy in South Africa: From *Black Hamlet* to *A Dream Deferred*', *Shakespeare in Southern Africa* 27 (2015): 1–14.

Schalkwyk, David. *Hamlet's Dreams: The Robben Island Shakespeare* (London: Bloomsbury, 2013).

Thurman, Chris. 'Accentism, Anglocentrism, and Multilingualism in South African Shakespeares' in *Shakespeare and Accentism*, ed. Adele Lee (London: Routledge, 2020), pp. 100–120.

———. 'Kunene and the Swan: Two Approaches to Biography, History and Shakespeare in South African Theatre', *Recherche littéraire / Literary Research* 36 (2020): 65–96.

———. 'Shakespeare.za: Digital Shakespeares and Education in South Africa', *Research in Drama Education* 25.1 (2020): 49–67.

CHAPTER 4

Practicing Digital Shakespeare in Latin America: Case Studies from Argentina and Brazil

Amrita Sen

Abstract This chapter looks at two distinct but connected websites—*Fundación Shakespeare Argentina* and the "Shakespeare in Brazil" section of the *MIT Global Shakespeares*—that are aimed at making globally accessible the performances and textual translations from Latin America. This chapter argues that these websites open up new possibilities of community building through their curatorial strategies and social outreach. They not only act as repositories of actual performances, but also function as archives of communal memories. Through bi-lingual records of social media exchanges and transcriptions of performances, they open up new possibilities of accessing and reading Latin American Shakespeares. This chapter interrogates the global relevance of these websites by taking into consideration the often overlooked history of Shakespeare transmission in Latin America.

A. Sen (✉)
University of Calcutta, Kolkata, India
e-mail: dr.amritasen.earlymodern@gmail.com

Keywords *Fundación Shakespeare Argentina* · *MIT Global Shakespeares* · Latin American Shakespeares

If the internet is a great democratizing tool, then curated scholarly or educational websites play a special role in highlighting Shakespeare appropriations from regions outside of metropolitan centers of the Global North. This chapter looks at two websites—*Fundación Shakespeare Argentina* and the "Shakespeare in Brazil" section of the *MIT Global Shakespeares Video & Performance Archive*—to show how they help build digital communities by addressing both regional concerns and questions of broader global outreach. The *Fundación Shakespeare Argentina* (*FSA*) completed ten years in May 2021; and while the core of the *Global Shakespeares* archive, the *Shakespeare Performance in Asia* (SPIA) was launched in 2009, the section on Brazil is more recent. The two websites, though different in their content and context share a common goal of making visible Latin American Shakespeare adaptations. Both websites open up new possibilities of community-building through their curatorial strategies and social outreach. They not only act as repositories of actual performances, but also function as archives of communal memories. *FSA* and *Global Shakespeares* are also more immediately connected to one another through the performance videos and scholarly expertise they share on each other's websites via hyperlinks. Thus together they form part of a digital public sphere that brings Latin American Shakespeares in conversation with other Global Shakespeares.

To speak of Shakespeares in Latin America, is to, of course, recognize a plurality of cultural contexts and histories.[1] As Alfredo Michel Modenessi points out, "Latin American countries are grouped under one denominator due to historic factors, including our endless status as 'developing nations' plagued by conflict, exploitation, and oppression, domestic and foreign, after independence from the empires presiding over three centuries of miscegenation, marginalization, mythologization."[2] Shakespeare transmission and adaptation in the region is thus equally diverse. Beginning with the nineteenth century, performances and translations of Shakespeare began to appear, particularly in Argentina and Brazil. Recent

---

[1] See for instance Santos, "Mestizo Shakespeares: A Study of Cultural Exchange," 11.

[2] Modenessi, "'You say you want a revolution?' Shakespeare in Mexican [dis]guise," 38.

volumes such as *Latin American Shakespeares* (2005) and *Shakespeare and Latinidad* (2021) have helped bring to the forefront not only the long history of Shakespeare reception and adaptation in Latin America but also the continued relevance of the bard within contemporary Latinx communities. Still, Latin American adaptations remain overlooked in comparison to some of the other geographies within the Global South. Moreover, as Modenessi and Ruben Espinosa argue, Latinx representations within theatrical or cinematic adaptations located in London or Hollywood tend to uphold stereotypes that broaden the "Shakespeare-Latinx divide."[3]

In this context digital platforms can be particularly useful in showcasing Latin American Shakespeare adaptations and scholarship to a broader global audience, thereby helping dispel many of these stereotypes. The two websites that this chapter uses as case studies—the *FSA* and "Shakespeare in Brazil" in *MIT Global Shakespeares*—are distinct. *MIT Global Shakespeares* sees itself principally as a video archive, while the FSA is more amorphous, spreading news and recording the latest Shakespeare-related activities from Argentina. At the same time, the two sites share common goals—of making accessible a rich diversity of Shakespeare appropriations. They both profess clearly outlined educational goals, and curate essays and resource materials. As such, the two sites raise interesting questions for us on the expanding digital frontiers of Global Shakespeares. How do these sites balance local and global concerns? How might we begin to understand these sites not only from within the context of Shakespeare studies but also from the perspective of decoloniality that lies at the heart of Global Shakespeares projects? This chapter examines *FSA* and "Shakespeare in Brazil" (and by extension the *MIT Global Shakespeares*) as sites of decoloniality. It reads the websites through two connected lenses— that of cultural anthropophagy and the decolonial archive—to show how *FSA* and "Shakespeare in Brazil" address issues of Shakespeare appropriation and community-building from outside of metropolitan centers of the Global North.

[3] Espinosa, "'Don't It Make My Brown Eyes Blue': Uneasy Assimilation and the Shakespeare-Latinx Divide," 89; see also Modenessi.

Digital Cultural Anthropophagy
and *Fundación Shakespeare Argentina*

The *Fundación Shakespeare Argentina* which celebrated its tenth anniversary in the middle of the pandemic, was set up as a non-profit dedicated to "deepening the knowledge, enjoyment, appreciation and spreading of the life and works of William Shakespeare in Argentina."[4] As a bi-lingual website, accessible in both Spanish and English, the *FSA* in many ways addresses questions of audience diversity, and attempts to balance regional users of its resources with global ones. One of the key features of the *FSA* website is its dynamic design that makes it more obviously user-friendly and navigable than its static counterparts. The *FSA* sets out to promote not only Shakespeare performances including those by its own troupe, the Compañía de Repertorio de la Fundación Shakespeare Argentina, but also makes available a wide range of educational tools. With the onset of the pandemic, the *FSA* has been part of global endeavors to keep theaters alive online. For instance, *FSA* directors Mercedes de la Torre and Carlos Drocchi collaborated on the live-streamed reading of *Much Ado About Nothing* on the web-series *The Show Must Go Online* started by the British actor Robert Myles. *The Show Must Go Online* was a response to the closure of the physical theaters because of the pandemic, and live-streamed readings of Shakespeare's plays in the order in which they appear in the *First Folio*. The series is available for free on YouTube.[5] The FSA also made available its production of *Much Ado About Nothing* on the online theater platform TEATRIX from March 2020.

The *FSA*'s pandemic response, that of accessing multiple global platforms, is not a novelty, but in fact an inherent aspect of how the website has been operating over the past decade. Its approach is what might best be described as digital cultural anthropophagy. Derived from the Brazilian modernist poet Oswald de Andrade's *Manifesto Antropófago* (*Cannibalist Manifesto*) (1928), cultural anthropophagy "describes a resistant method to absorb information from First World countries without losing cultural autonomy."[6] It is, therefore, a decolonial response to European cultural

---

[4] *Fundación Shakespeare Argentina*, https://shakespeareargentina.org/en/about-us/.

[5] *The Show Must Go Online*.

[6] Santos, 11.

hegemony, a response that does not however, foreclose European influences, but rather assumes a position of power and agency during such discursive exchanges. As Leslie Barry observes, as a methodology cultural anthropophagy "neither apes nor rejects European culture, but 'devours' it, adapting its strengths and incorporating them into the native self."[7] As a model of hybridity or even of creolization, cultural anthropophagy conveys a hunger to engage with the world, a methodology that imbibes the alien or the other from a position of conscious volition. In his *Manifesto Antropófago*, Andrade had early on made Shakespeare complicit, alluding to *Hamlet* is his now well-known quip "Tupi, or not tupi, that is the question."[8] Andrade here combines Hamlet's existentialist dilemma with the Tupi Indians of the Brazilian coast who were known for their cannibalistic practices. The line appears in English in the original 1928 version, and is an example of precisely the cultural cannibalism that Andrade was advocating. What is particularly appealing in the way that Andrade and others understand and advocate cultural anthropophagy is the way in which it includes the indigenous with the global, the regional with the cosmopolitan.[9] While cultural anthropophagy has been particularly influential within Latin American contexts, as recent titles such as *Eating Shakespeare: Cultural Anthropophagy as Global Methodology* (2019) prove, scholars from across the globe are waking up to its cannibalistic possibilities. For Global Shakespeares in particular, cultural anthropophagy offers an important critical tool for understanding the continued relevance of the Bard in the post-colonies.[10]

The *FSA* website organizes itself around the rubrics of "Activities, Education, Shakespeare, Argentina, Library, Company and News." In each subsection the *FSA* voraciously devours global influences. For instance, the section under "Library" contains links to Stanley Wells' lecture series posted on the Shakespeare Birthplace Trust Website. But it also contains audio and videos of FSA's own interviews with a wide range of international scholars and artists including Alexa Alice Joubin,

---

[7] Barry, "Oswald de Andrade's 'Cannibalist Manifesto'," 36.

[8] Andrade, 'Cannibalist Manifesto,' 38.

[9] Young, *Shakespeare in the Global South* 131; Camati, "Tupi or Not Tupi, That Is the Question," 123–124.

[10] Refskou, Carvalho and Amorim, "Introduction."

Sheila T. Cavanagh, Irina Brook, and William Sutton. The *FSA* importantly connects with other digital projects such as *MIT Global Shakespeares* and the *World Shakespeare Project* (*WSP*). The partnership programs of the *FSA* and *WSP* are detailed under the "Education" section and provide a much needed counterfoil to *WSP*'s own portal.[11] For instance, the video and image archives from 2019 document how students and faculty of Escuela de Lenguas Modernas, Universidad del Salvador (USAL) were part of *WSP*'s global digital learning community on Shakespeare that started well before the pandemic.[12] Older pages help document the long association of *FSA* and *WSP* over the years, and double up as a digital archive of the collaborative potential of Global Shakespeare projects, particularly those that have strong online components. As the *FSA* page clarifies regarding its partnership with *WSP*, "[t]hrough these international projects, the FSA forges and strengthens bonds with the educational community, contributing therefore to the knowledge, spreading and integration of our country to the rest of the world."[13]

It is through these collaborations and digital links that the *FSA* participates in the building of a virtual Shakespeare community. In the process it also connects the world to developments in adaptation and pedagogy in Argentina. One of the important resources that the *FSA* showcases is its interview with the late Argentinian artist, poet, and critic Rafael Squirru. Amongst his many accomplishments, Squirru was known for spearheading the establishment of the Buenos Aires Museum of Modern Art. He had also translated some of Shakespeare's sonnets and three of his plays—*Hamlet*, *The Tempest*, and *Romeo and Juliet*—although the last remains unpublished. The translations were illustrated by surrealist painter Juan Carlos Liberti, and links to Squirru's website enables one to see samples of these remarkable images. The other important set of resources that *FSA* offers, although they are not curated under a single heading are the

---

[11] The WSP directed by Sheila T. Cavanagh connects students at Emory University with students from partner institutions from across the globe using innovative digital technologies. The WSP website contains details of these student and faculty exchanges, including images and videos. However, not all the partner institutions, especially those from the Global South, offer parallel digital archives on their own websites documenting their experiences of these transcontinental Shakespeare classes. For more on WSP see Cavanagh.

[12] FSA, "WSP In Argentina 2019."

[13] FSA, "World Shakespeare Project in Argentina."

writings on and by Jorge Luis Borges. These include Borges' own essays on Shakespeare—"William Shakespeare: Teatro-Poesia Biografia," "La Cuestión Shakespeare," "El Teatro," "El Lenguaje de Shakespeare," "El Destino de Shakespeare," and his short story "Everything and Nothing." These form important counterparts to the other more familiar short story by Borges on the bard, namely, "La Memoria de Shakespeare" ("Shakespeare's Memory"). Borges had famously stated "if I think and think of Shakespeare, I think of a multitude,"[14] and the bard appears repeatedly in his own poems, stories, essays, and interviews. As Grace Tiffany observes "Borges's writings present a Shakespeare who, unlike Borges himself, could make the godlike sacrifice of his individual identity for the imagined lives of his characters."[15] Borges' writings explore the many facets of Shakespeare—as a dramatist but also as an English literary icon who has assumed global significance. The *FSA* seems to take on Borges' mantle— "With the same free spirit with which Borges exalts the great English writer, the Fundación Shakespeare Argentina specifies what is its task of dissemination [...]"[16] Channeling this Borgesian spirit, the *FSA* embraces the plural—it reaches out globally to performances, projects, translations.

What further accentuates FSA's global reach is its active utilization of social media. Its bi-lingual twitter feed embedded in the website further opens up possibilities of accessing and reading Latin American Shakespeares within a global context. But it is also actively present on Facebook, Vimeo, Instagram, Flickr, and Pinterest. As the long list of congratulatory videos, tweets, and messages celebrating the FSA's ten years attest, the website while disseminating local Argentinian Shakespeares, has succeeded in reaching a broader global audience.

[14] Enguidanos et al., "Now I am More or Less Who I am," 165.

[15] Tiffany, "Borges and Shakespeare, Shakespeare and Borges," 147.

[16] Melgarejo, "Borges, Shakespeare y la divulgación del arte."

PERFORMANCE ARCHIVES, BRAZIL, AND *MIT GLOBAL SHAKESPEARES*

The *MIT Global Shakespeares Video & Performance Archive* is an evolving archive. It draws its roots from the MIT Shakespeare Project that was started by Peter S. Donaldson in 1992.[17] But it also builds upon *Shakespeare Performance in Asia* (SPIA) and its impressive database of "more than forty hours of video recording of complete performances of Shakespeare plays and adaptations in a wide variety of genres, forms, and languages" compiled by Alexa Alice Joubin.[18] *Global Shakespeares* has expanded its scope to now include dedicated sections on East and Southeast Asia, India, Brazil, Europe, and the Arab World. As a collaborative project, it draws upon the expertise of scholars from across the world. The regional pages, moreover, have their own editors. As an archive *Global Shakespeares* showcases not only videos of performances but additional materials such as introductions, essays, scripts, glossary, and bibliography. These seem to fit in well with the archive's aim to "serve as a core resource for students, teachers, and researchers."[19]

As opposed to YouTube, which Stephen O'Neill for instance describes as an "accidental archive,"[20] and Christy Desmet brands as "the quintessential crowd-sourced site,"[21] *Global Shakespeares* is a scholarly, curated site. As a self-professed archive, *Global Shakespeares* has understandably generated discussions on exactly what sort of a digital archive it is; and by extension on the very nature of *any* digital archive. Desmet, for instance, argues: "[t]he online archive is a hybrid creature, located ambivalently within a spectrum of three organizational structures: the database, the archive, and the collection."[22] While a database sorts data, the archive becomes a repository, and the collection offers a glimpse of an arranged form of "whole" data.[23] The online archive itself, however has generated much debate amongst archival scholars in regard to how

---

[17] Trettein, "Shakespeares's Globe Goes *Global Shakespeares*," 155.

[18] Joubin, "Online Media Report," 245.

[19] *MIT Global Shakespeares*, "About the Archive."

[20] O'Neill, *Shakespeare and YouTube*, 11.

[21] Christy Desmet, "The Art of Curation."

[22] Ibid.

[23] Ibid.

it might be understood viz-a-viz traditional brick and mortar archives. While online archives are often distinguished on the basis of whether they are the digitized products of analog collections, or are born digital (repositories of materials that only have virtual existence), archivists like Kate Theimer for instance ask for a further distinction between "digital archives" and "digital historical representations" such as databases and Google Books.[24] Theimer in fact remains skeptical as to whether all digital archives can at all be deemed equal to traditional archives.[25] Even for advocates of online archives, it is their hybridity that stands out; a hybridity that is understood in multiple ways. For Kenneth Price, coordinator of the Walt Whitman Archive, online archives, especially scholarly ones "blends features of editing and archiving."[26] The online archive pushes at the boundaries of what we have traditionally understood as archival space and archival practice.

The archive, of course, has always been a contested space. Jacques Derrida traces the origins of the archive to *arkhē* or commandment and also to *arkheion* or the residence of the commanding magistrates.[27] It was in the house of the *archons*, the law-makers, that the "official documents [were] filed."[28] As Derrida elaborates "The archons are first of all the documents' guardians. [...] They are also accorded the hermeneutic right and competence. They have the power to interpret the archives."[29] The archive, is therefore, linked with questions of power, authority, and access. For postcolonial scholars, the archive raises other related questions—those of inclusion and silence.[30] While Derrida speaks of the violence of the archive, Walter Mignolo for instance highlights the violence of the colonial archive. Writing of museums as "places where the western archive was enacted" Mignolo highlights how they "were also the place to collect and organize artefacts of the non-European world – collected artifacts, but not

---

[24] Theimer, "A Distinction Worth Exploring."

[25] Ibid.; see also Clement et al. "Toward a Notion of the Archive of the Future," 112.

[26] Price, "Edition, Project, Database, Archive, Thematic Research Collection"; Clement et al., 113.

[27] Derrida, 2.

[28] Ibid.

[29] Ibid.

[30] See for instance Spivak, "The Rani of Sirmur: An Essay in Reading the Archives"; Stoler, *Along the Archival Grain*.

the memories of the people from where the artefacts were removed, either by looting or purchasing."[31] The result is an archival silence, an absence of crucial memories and narratives. For Mignolo, as for other scholars of postcolonial studies the process of decolonization becomes important in confronting and countering these silences of the archive. As Catherine E. Walsh and Mignolo argue in their introduction to *On Decoloniality: Concepts, Analytics, Praxis* (2018) "decoloniality undoes, disobeys, and delinks from this matrix; constructing paths and praxis toward an otherwise of thinking, sensing, believing, doing, and living."[32] Here I wish to read *MIT Global Shakespeares* and its "Shakespeare in Brazil" section as an attempt at decolonizing the Shakespeare archive.

Modenessi in a recent essay calls out the "neo-exoticist trumpetry" of a production of *Much Ado About Nothing* at London's Globe Theatre in 2017. Critiquing the casual misappropriation of Latin American (in this context Mexican) history and cultural markers by the Globe production, Modenessi praises local productions such as Los Colochos' *Mendoza* (Macbeth) for a more "thoughtful articulation of Shakespeare's art and themes with Mexico's realities and artistry."[33] What Modenessi highlights is symptomatic of the larger problem of cultural misappropriation or even cultural tourism that is often seen in theatrical and cinematic productions from metropolitan centers. Digital archives (much like online repositories that Heidi Craig and Laura Estill write about in their chapter) can offer a counter to what Modenessi describes as "hegemonic" appropriation, by making productions from the Global South visible. If the colonial archive silences the non-metropolitan voices, then the decolonial archive attempts to restore the plurality of memories, experiences, and histories. By making available many of the performances and cinematic adaptations from peripheral geographies *Global Shakespeares* thus constructs an archive that challenges the colonial logic.[34] Curated by scholars from regions, the website moreover makes visible their critical labor while also building an inclusive global community centered around Shakespeare appropriation and scholarship.

---

[31] Mignolo, "Enacting the Archives."

[32] Walsh and Mignolo, "Introduction," 4.

[33] Modenessi, 37.

[34] Not all the entries on the *Global Shakespeares* site have full videos owing to copyright issues, but many of them do. Even when full videos are unavailable selected clips often are.

"Shakespeare in Brazil" is one of the major regions covered by *MIT Global Shakespeares* and is curated by Anna Stegh Camati, Cristiane Busato Smith, and Liana Leão. The section is introduced by its three regional editors who provide a much needed history of Shakespeare transmission in Brazil. It in fact compliments the separate "Shakespeare in Latin America" essay by Aimara da Cunha Resende that is available on the *MIT Global Shakespeares* site. At the time of writing this chapter in 2021, the section on Brazil has 39 videos of performances. In comparison, East and Southeast Asia has 72 videos, Europe 45, the Arab World 20, and India around 19. Outside of *Global Shakespeares'* own regional emphasis areas, Argentina has videos from around 4 productions, while Colombia and Uruguay have one each. Brazil, is therefore, better represented than some of the other regions and countries in this growing archive.

The videos from the Brazil section are mostly of stage performances, as opposed to those for instance from India which are a mix of theater and film clips. This rich selection of theatrical performances form an invaluable resource and the production notes provided by the regional editors not only make these more accessible to a global audience but can also double up as useful teaching resources. One of the key features of the *MIT Global Shakespeares* is how metadata is managed, and in the "Shakespeare in Brazil" this becomes especially useful in tagging theater companies. A group of the performances curated on the site are by the Cia. Rústica (Rustic Theatre Company) from the city of Porto Alegre in Rio Grande do Sul in Southern Brazil.[35] The three productions, *Macbeth, Herói Bandido* (*Macbeth, the Bandit Hero*, 2004), *Sonho de Uma Noite de Verao* (*A Midsummer Night's Dream*, 2006), and *A Megera Domada* (*The Taming of the Shrew*, 2008), all directed by Patrícia Fagundes were part of a project called the "In Search of Shakespeare" ("Em busca de Shakespeare").[36] The productions of the Cia. Rústica are marked by their minimalist stages and musicality. In *A Megera Domada* the use of unisex clothes by the actors at the beginning of the play further add to tensions in the prescribed gender roles of Shakespeare's characters. While *Sonho de Uma Noite de Verao* also has a bare stage, the lighting strategies, costumes, and most of all the music bring about a dream-like quality.

[35] Camati, *A Megera Domada (The Taming of the Shrew)*.
[36] Ibid.

Fig. 4.1 *Bruxas da Escócia* (*The Witches from Scotland*) by Cia Vagalum Tum Tum (Courtesy: *MIT Global Shakespeares*)

The music and dialogue accompany each other throughout the production, the former adding new layers of meaning to the Shakespearean text. Camati draws attention to what she describes as the "intermediality" of Fagundes' adaptation that brings together "different dance rhythms, such as the *tango, bolero, samba,* jazz, blues, *passo doble, bossa nova,* among others, composed for the musical arias, duets and choruses" in addition to influences from Broadway and Hollywood.[37] The cabaret that drives the music as well as the dance, allows Fagundes to tease out differing characters and their erotic desires (Fig. 4.1).

In contrast, the Cia Vagalum Tum Tum productions featured in the archive are meant for children. With colorful backdrop, elaborate make-up, costumes, and music the Company transforms Shakespeare's greatest tragedies into comic performances for a younger audience. *Othelito* (2007), *O Bobo do Rei* (*The King's Fool,* 2010), *O Principe da Dinamarca* (*The Prince of Denmark* 2011), *Bruxas da Escócia* (*The Witches from Scotland,* 2014), all directed by Ângelo Brandini, use aspects of

---

[37] Camati, "IntermedIal performance AesthetIcs In PatrícIa Fagundes' A Midsummer Night's Dream," 149.

commedia dell'arte, clowning, and acrobatics.[38] In *O Príncipe da Dinamarca* (*Hamlet*) for instance, it is the skeletons in the graveyard that tell the stories of their violent deaths through clowning. The *Bruxas da Escócia* (*Macbeth*) goes for a colorful retelling, with the roles of Macbeth and Lady Macbeth being played by women. Tereza Gontijo as Macbeth and Christiane Galvan as Lady Macbeth add comic dimensions to the characters but also implicitly engage with questions of gender roles and effeminacy that the play raises. Instead of murdering Duncan with a dagger, a switch is flipped on the throne—the king disappears and his cardboard cut-out is carried out. That this intrepid mechanism works is first tested out on a Teddy Bear by Macbeth and Lady Macbeth. Later, puppets are used to stand in for Macbeth's new subjects. The adaptation, available as a wonderful resource for introducing children to Shakespeare, also encourages scholars to think of the bard's performances outside of usual adult audiences.

Many of the videos under "Shakespeare in Brazil" come with tags to other global performances. *O Príncipe da Dinamarca* for instance points one to other adaptations of *Hamlet*—the Tibetan film *Prince of the Himalayas* (2006), Shanghai Peking Opera's *The Tragedy of Prince Zi Dan* (*Revenge of the Prince*, 2006), Shanghai Yueju Company's *Wangzi fuchou ji* (*The Revenge of the Prince*, 1994). This allows for a much needed comparative perspective of the bard's plays. It also facilitates comparison amongst plays produced within Brazil. For instance, Cia Rústica's *Megera Domada* leads one to *A Megera Domada de Rua* (*The Street Taming of the Shrew*, 2009). Performed by Ueba Produtos Notáveis, a street company from Rio Grande do Sul, *The Street Taming of the Shrew* relies on actors to enact multiple roles, and utilizes masks and dolls to accommodate the lack of a formal stage. The "Shakespeare in Brazil" section thus showcases a truly wide selection of performances and critical notes that reveal the rich tradition of Shakespeare appropriation.

CONCLUSION

Digital media can make visible and accessible Shakespeare appropriations from hitherto overlooked cultural contexts. They can simultaneously reach out to local and global audiences. The *FSA* and "Shakespeare in

---

[38] Camati, *Bruxas da Escócia*.

Brazil" as part of *MIT Global Shakespeares* belong to a new phase of Global Shakespeares, reaching out to a new generation of Shakespeare users. Like other open access curated sites from the Global South such as *Shakespeare ZA* or *Shakespeare in Bengal* that are discussed elsewhere in this collection, they perform multiple functions—as repositories of actual performances or memories of past performances, educational tools, and disseminators of news and events related to Shakespeare appropriations. Bilingual sites such as the *FSA*, moreover, can reach out to a larger global community. Simultaneously using social media tools, these largely educational websites offer important and viable alternatives to non-curated sites such as YouTube.

References

Andrade, Oswald de. "Cannibalist Manifesto." Trans. Leslie Barry. *Latin American Literary Review*. Vol. 19, No. 38 (Jul.–Dec., 1991), pp. 38–47.

Barry, Leslie. "Oswald de Andrade's 'Cannibalist Manifesto'." *Latin American Literary Review*. Vol. 19, No. 38 (Jul.–Dec., 1991), pp. 35–37.

Boffone, Trevor and Carla Della Gata. *Shakespeare and Latinidad*. Edinburgh: Edinburgh University Press, 2021.

Camati, Anna Stegh. "*A Midsummer Night's Dream*: Patricia Fagundes' Intermedial Performance Aesthetics." *Aletria*. Vol. 23, No. 3 (2013), pp. 141–156.

———. *Bruxas da Escócia*. *MIT Global Shakespeares Video & Performance Archive*. https://globalshakespeares.mit.edu/bruxas-da-escocia-brandini-angelo-2014/#video=bruxas-da-escocia-brandini-angelo-2014. Accessed November 30, 2021.

———. "'Tupi or Not Tupi, That Is the Question': Brazilian Mythical Afterlives of Shakespeare's *Hamlet*." *Local and Global Myths in Shakespearean Performance*. Ed. Aneta Mancewicz and Alexa Alice Joubin. New York: Palgrave Macmillan, 2018.

Camati, Anna Stegh, Cristiane Busato Smith, and Liana Leão. "Shakespeare in Brazil." *MIT Global Shakespeares Video & Performance Archive*. https://globalshakespeares.mit.edu/brazil/. Accessed October 20, 2021.

Clement, Tanya, Wendy Hagenmaier and Jennie Levine Knies, "Toward a Notion of the Archive of the Future: Impressions of Practice by Librarians, Archivists, and Digital Humanities Scholars." *The Library Quarterly: Information, Community, Policy*. Vol. 83, No. 2 (April 2013), pp. 112–130.

Derrida. Jacques. *Archive Fever: A Freudian Impression*. Trans. Eric Prenowitz. Chicago: The University of Chicago Press, 1996.

Desmet, Christy. "The Art of Curation: Searching for Global Shakespeares in the Digital Archives." Special Issue on "Global Shakespeares in World Markets and Archives." Ed. Alexa Alice Joubin. *Borrowers and Lenders: The Journal of Shakespeare and Appropriation.* Vol. 11. No. 1 (Oct 2017). https://openjournals.libs.uga.edu/borrowers/article/view/2411/2490.

Enguidanos, Miguel, et al. "Now I am More or Less Who I am." *Jorge Luis Borges: Conversation.* Ed. Richard Burgin. Jackson: University Press of Mississippi Press, 1998.

Espinosa, Ruben. "'Don't It Make My Brown Eyes Blue': Uneasy assimilation and the Shakespeare-Latinx Divide." *The Routledge Handbook of Shakespeare and Global Appropriation.* Ed. Christy Desmet, Sujata Iyengar and Miriam Jacobson. New York: Routledge, 2019.

Fundación Shakespeare Argentina. https://shakespeareargentina.org/en/. Accessed November 24, 2021.

———. "WSP In Argentina 2019." https://shakespeareargentina.org/en/wsp-in-argentina-2019/.

———. "World Shakespeare Project in Argentina." https://shakespeareargentina.org/en/world-shakespeare-project-in-argentina/.

Joubin, Alexa Alice. "Online Media Report: 'Global Shakespeares and Shakespeare Performance in Asia:' Open-Access Digital Video Archives." *Asian Theatre Journal.* Vol. 28, No. 1 (Spring 2011), pp. 244–250.

Melgarejo, Graciela. "Borges, Shakespeare y la divulgación del arte" ("Borges, Shakespeare and the Dissemination of Art"). Rpt. *Fundación Shakespeare Argentina.* https://shakespeareargentina.org/en/borges-shakespeare-y-la-divulgacion-del-arte-fsa-10-years-article-by-graciela-melgarejo/. Accessed November 24, 2021.

Mignolo. Walter D. "Enacting the Archives, Decentring the Muses: The Museum of Islamic Art in Doha and the Asian Civilizations Museum in Singapore." *Ibraaaz.* Vol 6 (November 2013). https://www.ibraaz.org/essays/77. Accessed November 24, 2021.

MIT Global Shakespeares Video & Performance Archive. https://globalshakespeares.mit.edu/. Accessed November 24, 2021.

Modenessi, Alfredo Michel. "'You Say You Want a Revolution?' Shakespeare in Mexican [dis]guise." *The Routledge Handbook of Shakespeare and Global Appropriation.* Ed. Christy Desmet, Sujata Iyengar and Miriam Jacobson. New York: Routledge, 2019.

O'Neill, Stephen. *Shakespeare and YouTube: New Media Forms of the Bard.* London: Bloomsbury Publishing, 2014.

Price, Kenneth M. "Edition, Project, Database, Archive, Thematic Research Collection: What's in a Name?" *Digital Humanities Quarterly.* Vol. 3, No. 3 (2009). http://www.digitalhumanities.org/dhq/vol/3/3/000053/000053.html.

Refskou, Anne Sophie, Marcel Alvaro de Amorim and Vinicius Mariano de Carvalho. "Introduction." *Eating Shakespeare: Cultural Anthropophagy as Global Methodology*. London: Bloomsbury Publishing, 2019.

Santos, Rick J. "Mestizo Shakespeares: A Study of Cultural Exchange." *Latin American Shakespeares*. Ed. Bernice W. Kliman and Rick J. Santos. Madison: Farleigh Dickinson University Press, 2005.

Spivak, Gayatri Chakravorty. "The Rani of Sirmur: An Essay in Reading the Archives." *History and Theory*. Vol. 24, No. 3 (1985), 247–272. https://doi.org/10.2307/2505169.

Stoler, Ann Laura. *Along the Archival Grain: Epistemic Anxieties and Colonial Common Sense*. Princeton: Princeton University, Press, 2009.

The Show Must Go Online. https://robmyles.co.uk/theshowmustgoonline/. Accessed November 24, 2021.

Theimer, Kate. "A Distinction Worth Exploring: 'Archives' and 'Digital Historical Representations.'" *Journal of Digital Humanities*. Vol. 3. No. 2 (2014). http://journalofdigitalhumanities.org/3-2/a-distinction-worth-exploring-archives-and-digital-historical-representations/. Accessed November 21, 2021.

Tiffany, Grace. "Borges and Shakespeare, Shakespeare and Borges." *Latin American Shakespeares*. Ed. Bernice W. Kliman and Rick J. Santos. Madison: Farleigh Dickinson University Press, 2005.

Trettien, Whitney Anne. "Shakespeare's Globe Goes *Global Shakespeares*." *The Shakespearean International Yearbook*. Vol. 14. Special Section, Digital Shakespeares. Ed. Brett D. Hirsch and Hugh Craig. Burlington: Ashgate, 2014.

Walsh, Catherine E. and Walter D. Mignolo, "Introduction." *On Decoloniality: Concepts, Analytics, Praxis*. Ed. Walter D. Mignolo and Catherine E. Walsh. Durham: Duke University Press, 2018.

Young, Sandra. *Shakespeare in the Global South*. London: Bloomsbury Publishing, 2019.

CHAPTER 5

Teaching Shakespeare in the Indian (Google) Classroom: The Digital Promise and the Digital Divide

Souvik Mukherjee

Abstract Mukherjee's chapter attempts to view the nascent online Shakespeare teaching in India within the context of the centuries-old traditions of Shakespeare pedagogy in the country. In doing so, he traces a connect with the colonial pedagogy and its post-independence forms with the current online avatar, especially from post-Covid times. While addressing the more commonly advertised narrative of technological promise, this chapter also points out how, as in the early days of the East India Company, Shakespeare still belongs to an elite, only one that is larger in number—even with greater connectivity and global reach, access remains limited and is a matter of privilege as is especially evident from the digital divide in India in post-Covid times.

Keywords Digital divide · Coronavirus pandemic · Indian Shakespeares

S. Mukherjee (✉)
Centre for Studies in Social Sciences, Calcutta, Kolkata, India
e-mail: prosperoscell@gmail.com

A. Sen (ed.), *Digital Shakespeares from the Global South*, Global Shakespeares, https://doi.org/10.1007/978-3-031-04787-9_5

SHAKESPEARE IN INDIA: FROM MACAULAY TO WHATSAPP

The only thing that Thomas Babington Macaulay liked about his stay in India is embodied in his comment made to Captain David Lester Richardson, who taught English in and was later principal of the Hindoo College in Calcutta: "I may forget everything about India but your reading of Shakespeare, never".[1] When Macaulay drafted his "Minute on Education" in 1830, he was as good as his word and commented that "A single shelf of a good European library was worth the whole native literature of India and Arabia",[2] sealing the fate of Indian education for centuries and also, within it, that of Shakespeare. Shakespeare has been the major influence on Indian education from the days of the East India Company's rule and it is of little wonder that almost three centuries later, how Shakespeare is taught in India is of such paramount interest. The story of English literature teaching in India is the stuff of local legends about professors of heroic stature and even with the coming of the Covid-19 pandemic, when traditional classroom pedagogies have been retired, Shakespeare teaching has nevertheless continued bravely, albeit online. There are, of course, dissenting voices that question the relevance of Shakespeare in these changing times and pick up on the current irrelevance of the colonial intention of using Shakespeare as part of their "civilizing mission".[3] It is not surprising therefore that an essay on the online teaching of the Romantics or the Modernist poets in India will be difficult to find but Shakespeare pedagogy in India can confidently claim what it deems its rightful place even in the "brave new world" of the pandemic and its aftermath.

While it is necessary to start with the online teaching scenario during the pandemic, it is also important to look back at earlier work on online Shakespeare teaching and Shakespeare research in general in India. It should also be pointed out that despite Shakespeare's ubiquitous influence in schools, colleges and universities all over the country, online teaching

---

[1] Supriya Chaudhuri, "Remembering Shakespeare in India: Colonial and Postcolonial Memory," n.p. The Hindoo College was set up in 1817 as one of the first western style higher education institutions in Asia. It was later renamed Presidency College. In 2010 the college became Presidency University. This article will be using each of the three names reflective of the different stages of this institute's evolution.

[2] Macaulay, "Minute on Education (1835) by Thomas Babington Macaulay."

[3] For a detailed study on the colonial history of Shakespeare studies in India, its advocates and dissidents see Singh *Colonial Narratives/Cultural Dialogues*, 120–151.

and even Internet access are novelties for many and archival data is often difficult to come by. One of the key questions this chapter asks is, in the face of the pandemic and the consequent restructuring of pedagogies, what will be the role of the redoubtable Shakespeare pedagogy in the Indian educational system in the years to come? In addressing this question, it will also be important to establish the locus of India within the Global South in general in the way Shakespeare features in online pedagogies and scholarship. This chapter will first examine the complexities of online education in India, before situating digital Shakespeares within the longer and complex history of Shakespeare pedagogy in India. It will, moreover, draw upon interviews of college and university teachers and students to provide a more practical picture of how digital Shakespeares in India transitioned into the pandemic years.

The Internet, Shakespeare and India

Despite the second-highest number of Internet users in the world, a massive 624 million, the penetration of the Internet is relatively low, standing at 45%.[4] Despite the rapid progress from the Internet penetration five years ago, India still ranks 49th on the global Internet inclusivity index and it makes up for in affordability what it lacks in access. One could also add training and awareness of the digital possibilities to the tally as these became obvious when Covid-19 made academics the world over move towards online teaching. It is important to keep in mind, therefore, that many Indians have no access to the Internet and those who do are often not professionally trained in online learning and teaching.

Nevertheless, there is a surprisingly large number of Indian websites that are concerned with Shakespeare—these are either full-fledged academic databases or parts of such databases or they form a rather motley collection ranging from occasional mentions on websites to detailed feature articles. Examples of the latter include *The Times of India's* "Five Plays in Which Shakespeare Mentioned India"[5] or in a similar vein, *India Today's* "Do You Know What Shakespeare Wrote about India?"[6] and almost, as if to explain this deep involvement with Shakespeareana, a

[4] Keelery, "India: Internet Penetration Rate 2021."

[5] *The Times of India,* "5 plays in which Shakespeare mentioned India!"

[6] Ashok, "Do You Know What Shakespeare Wrote about India?"

feature article on Sir Francis Younghusband's essay on India's obsession with Shakespeare, reprinted in the popular online news site *Scroll.in* from the British Library's Asian and African Studies blog.[7] Besides, if one is to follow Thomas Kullman's methodology from his essay, "Shakespeare on the Internet", then there will be many more:

> One of the most salient features of this list is the wide variety of contexts in which the Hamlet phrases appear. We are by no means limited to the fields of arts and literature. Many of the hits concern websites devoted to specialised areas, such as economics, medicine, law and computing. In the areas of artistic and literary production, most of the hits indicate websites devoted to popular culture: TV, film series, comics and most persistently, pop songs.[8]

Such a list is, however, not what concerns this essay. Many of the types of borrowings that Kullman identifies here have more to do with the already extant centuries-long history of Shakespearean imports into the English vocabulary and phraseology.

The academic databases, however, are another matter. One of the examples is the famed video archive of Indian films and plays with Shakespearean connections curated by Poonam Trivedi that is part of the *MIT Global Shakespeare Project*. Folger Shakespeare Library's podcast on Shakespeare in India featuring an interview with Jyotsna G. Singh is another valuable addition as would be the numerous essays on the Internet database, *JSTOR*, which is now made accessible to Indian universities through the INFLIBNET network maintained by the Indian government. Jadavpur University's unique project, *Shakespeare in Bengal*, archives in much detail the Shakespeare pedagogy in post-independence India (and in some cases earlier) and also the theatrical performances of Shakespeare in eastern India. In the *Internet Shakespeare Editions* project supported by the University of Victoria, Canada, eminent Shakespeare scholar Sukanta Chaudhuri outlines the complexity and significance of "the Shakespearean presence in India":

---

[7] Waddell and Sutton, "Shakespeare in India: How Indians Saw and Read the Bard a Hundred Years Back."

[8] Kullman, "Shakespeare on the Internet: Global and South Asian Appropriations," 164.

Shakespeare provided the biggest single channel for not only literary or artistic innovations but the underlying transformation of values. 'Channel' is the wrong term. Traits and values were not merely imbibed through or from Shakespeare; to a much greater extent, Indian values and practices were implanted on or even evolved through his work. 'Shakespeare' became the appellation for a commodity and an ethos in a manner comparable only with developments in the West.[...] We are talking of at least a dozen languages and cultural regions, each ramifying into many social groups and artistic practices, over 200 years and more. We need to map a few paths through the maze: academic study, translation/adaptation, and performance. The paths intersect constantly and are sometimes hard to trace.[9]

To these already labyrinthine Shakespearean connections in India that Chaudhuri rightly points out, one now needs to add the equally complicated hypertextual connections of the Internet.

Shakespeare Pedagogy in India

A brief discussion on how Shakespeare has traditionally been taught in Indian classrooms will be useful here to better understand the later transition to online teaching modes. Chaudhuri lists names of eminent Shakespeare teachers in India, both English and Indian stating that they "provided the stuff of legends in the *guru*-oriented orthodoxy that still lingers in Indian academia".[10] In other words, the figure of the Shakespeare teacher in the traditional Indian classroom became almost as important as what was taught. Richardson, Henry Louis Vivian Derozio and their later successors Praphulla Chandra Ghosh, Taraknath Sen and Arunkumar Dasgupta, spanning the history of Kolkata's Shakespeare pedagogy from the early nineteenth century to the late twentieth century, fill the pages of the legends of Shakespeare teaching in West Bengal. Chaudhuri lists names from other parts of India: "V.K. Ayyappan Pillai, R. Krishnamurthy, K.D. Sethna, S. Nagarajan and S. Viswanathan in southern India (chiefly Chennai and Hyderabad); Phiroze Dustoor, Sarup Singh and A.N. Kaul in Delhi; V.Y. Kantak in Vadodara; and M.V.

---

[9] Sukanta Chaudhuri, "Shakespeare in India."
[10] Ibid.

Rajadhyaksha, Homai Shroff and Kamal Wood in Mumbai".[11] Chaudhuri himself, with his immense scholarship, also falls within the "stuff
of legends" as the adulation that this author has heard from as unlikely
a person as a vice-president of a corporate, to the posts of students on
social media testify.

The importance of Shakespeare in early colonial education is underscored by scholars such as Gauri Viswanathan in her *Masks of Conquest*,
where she notes that mainly because of missionary activities, from the
"1820s to the mid-1850S English literary studies had a predominantly
religious and moral function in the Indian curriculum".[12] Hema Dahiya,
however, in her recent thesis on Shakespeare education in early colonial
India rightly observes that Shakespeare was part of the colonial Indian
curricula and even pre-dated the Shakespeare teaching in the Hindoo
College (which was established in 1817). She cites Krishna Chandra Lahiri
as stating that "the students [in schools] were initiated into the works
of Shakespeare through the famous *Tales from Shakespeare* ... [which]
used to be universally read in schools and outside, and was as popular as
Grimm's *Fairy Tales* and Swift's *Gulliver's Travels*".[13] Dahiya contends
that, *pace* Vishwanathan, Shakespeare was viewed favorably in contemporary accounts on education in early colonial India. It is no surprise,
therefore, that with such a long history of teaching Shakespeare that is
possibly among the oldest in the world, Shakespeare would continue to be
indispensable to education in India, both during and after colonial rule.
Chaudhuri believes that Shakespeare teaching is mainly concentrated in
the metropolises but that "in India as a whole, despite a Shakespearean
presence in the curricula of most universities, serious academic interest
in Shakespeare seems to be on the decline"[14]; this, of course, is a moot
point given the slew of Bollywood and other regional films drawing on
Shakespeare's plays and his transmedial presence in a multitude of mass
media. Nevertheless, the divide in Shakespeare teaching and scholarship
has been pointed out by others as well; as eminent poet Arvind Krishna
Mehrotra comments, "Most of my students come from these adjoining
areas and many are the first generation in their families to learn English.

---

[11] Ibid.

[12] Viswanathan *Masks of Conquest*, 142.

[13] Dahiya, "Shakespeare Studies in Colonial Bengal: The Early Phase," 5.

[14] Sukanta Chaudhuri, n.p.

It is difficult to teach them Shakespeare or Shelley when they are barely familiar with the alphabet. Basically, they bring a textbook to class and you tell them a few things in Hindi".[15]

Digital projects such as *Shakespeare in Bengal* can also provide powerful insights into traditional pedagogic practices. In a series of interviews conducted among current faculty members from different parts of the country, the *Shakespeare in Bengal* team has compiled a valuable oral-history archive of Shakespeare pedagogy in India.[16] One of the questions asked was regarding how Shakespeare was taught and the responses, although varied, generally agree that the key emphasis was on reading the text with the students and "academic analysis of the text"; one of the respondents' comments that her professor "used to do a very close reading. Every word was important to him. He would explain every comma and period – why it was there. He tried to direct our attention to all the explanations a word could have".[17] Another respondent, highlighted how the professor kept her enthralled with his lectures on *Macbeth*. Although reference to Shakespeare performances was not usual, it seems that the professor's classroom performance played a major part in Shakespeare pedagogy. Many respondents have described the legendary Taraknath Sen's practice of trying to identify what he called the "short lines" in Shakespeare as being part of his teaching method. Later criticism has pointed out the "one-sidedness" of Sen's argument in that he did not consider the possibility of mislineation by the compositors.[18] The "stuff of legends" point made by Chaudhuri regarding those who taught Shakespeare is well taken. In another essay, Swapan Kumar Chakravorty notes that there was a hierarchy among teachers in his college (Presidency College, Calcutta) in the Seventies wherein only a select few would be allowed to teach Shakespeare and the even more elect would be allowed to teach the tragedies.[19] The hagiology of Indian Shakespeare teachers is a topic for another discussion but the pedagogical implications needed to be considered to trace the way in which digital pedagogy has developed around Shakespeare.

[15] Soofi, "Arvind Krishna Mehrotra: Allahabad's Prodigal Poet."

[16] "Shakespeare in Bengal."

[17] "Dhritikanta Lahiri Chowdhury & Sheila Lahiri Chowdhury."

[18] Walton, "Textual Studies" 158.

[19] Chakravorty, *Bangalir Engreji Sahitya Charcha*.

The Internet and Shakespeare Teaching in India

The Internet is a destroyer of mystique and awe. With millions of electronic books and journal articles available on websites, both legit and otherwise, and online courses offered on online universities and academies, the access to Shakespeare scholarship has become much greater in India in the past two decades as it has in most parts of the so-called Global South. More universities in the Global South provide access to JSTOR, EEBO, LION, ProQuest and other databases that stock early modern source material and critical scholarship. Digital piracy is also still very common and makes both books and journals available to a greater extent where universities do not have access; of course, scholars and students in India stand at a comparative disadvantage from their peers in the Global North because many books and journals still remain behind paywalls. Nevertheless, the much-increased access, easy searchability and the multimedia experience of the plays can make a considerable difference to pedagogy. Add to this, the online courses made available for free or at very low cost by Massive Open Online Course (MOOC) providers such as Coursera.com, the MIT (MITX), Harvard (EdX) and the Khan Academy. In India, SWAYAM, the government-run online course provider also makes available courses on Shakespeare such as the course "Shakespeare Across Cultures" run by the Central University of Kerala. In terms of databases and other kinds of multimedia teaching platforms, a few examples need to be cited. The *Shakespeare in Bengal* database that has been mentioned above is a rich repository of interviews with Shakespeare performance artists and with academics; it could be seen as a potentially useful tool for teaching Shakespeare and his reception in India. Poonam Trivedi's detailed archive of Shakespeare productions from India, for the *MIT Global Shakespeares Archive* is a similarly valuable digital teaching asset. The British Council's "Mix the Play" website where the user can "direct" a Shakespeare play by choosing the actor, the venue and other production parameters is an excellent way to introduce students to Shakespeare performances.[20] In fact, this would be a useful way to address the lacuna in Shakespeare teaching as described before, where Shakespeare's stagecraft was rarely discussed as reported in the interviews on Shakespeare pedagogy (*Shakespeare in Bengal*). In addition to such institutionalized modes of digital Shakespeare teaching, there

---

[20] British Council, "Mix The Play."

are of course numerous websites accessible to students, albeit of varying academic merit. As such, the Shakespeare teacher as a fount of wisdom or a legendary figure may have to bow out to the Internet. Further, as Kullman observes, Shakespeare is quite widely present on the Internet in non-academic websites, sometimes even bordering on the casual and the flippant, signifying a wider reach beyond the confines of academic discussion and theatrical performance.

In his study, Kullman sees the following as being the reasons behind the widespread presence of Shakespeare on the Internet (through various Shakespeare allusions that crop up in random spaces on the web):

- The cultural tradition, common to South Asia and Europe, of discussing unresolved societal issues in cultural artefacts, such as fiction and drama,
- A high degree of cultural literacy, that is an awareness of the significance of literary classics,
- A special relationship with the English Language (which certainly goes back to colonial practices) in the context of which studying English is not just purpose-oriented (as in other countries in which languages other than English are spoken) but also connected to studying literary texts, including Shakespeare,
- A high degree of familiarity with electronic media.[21]

His observations on the cultural tradition of discussing societal issues in cultural artefacts and on the high degree of cultural literacy are valid, of course but with certain qualifications. The "high degree of familiarity with electronic media" is a moot point, however, especially when one looks carefully at the Internet usage statistics, particularly from the perspective of demographic reach. As mentioned before, Statista.com reports a 45% Internet penetration statistic with 624 million users, a market second only to China in terms of numbers.[22] Nevertheless, in comparison to the population, the reach is shy of less than half of India's population. So over 55% of the population of India cannot reach any information, let alone Shakespeare's works, online. Of these, the larger concentrations of users are near New Delhi while states such as Odisha have a much lower Internet

[21] Kullman, "Shakespeare on the Internet."

[22] Keelery, "India: Internet Penetration Rate 2021."

access. About 91.7% users access the Internet via their mobiles so even if there is an overlap with those who access it via computers, phones remain the primary gadgets. These technical specifications should also be kept in mind while designing digital Shakespeares. For example, consider the British Council's "Mix the Play" website. On a mobile phone (and the author was using a 9-inch phone with 4 GB RAM), it can only be run on a smartphone with Android or IOS and that too in landscape mode. Feature phone users cannot access it and others who do not have the required high-end processing power on their phones will struggle to make it work. Although the average download speeds are listed as relatively high in the statistical charts, personal experience says otherwise, especially when traveling to non-urban locations. Consider the gender divide in accessing mobile Internet and another perspective opens up: "Indian women are 15 percent less likely to own a mobile phone, and 33 percent less likely to use mobile internet services than men. In 2020, 25 percent of the total adult female population owned a smartphone versus 41 percent of adult men".[23] A few more points need to be taken into account before one can make any sweeping claim for a high level of familiarity with digital media:

> This gendered digital divide is often born out of a triple disadvantage for women in India. First, there is a rural-urban digital divide, such that rural broadband penetration is only 29 percent against a national average of 51 percent. Across states, women in rural areas are less likely to own mobile phones, with this rural-urban divide being the narrowest in Goa, Kerala, and North-eastern states, and the widest in West Bengal, Gujarat, Maharashtra, Andhra Pradesh, and Telangana. Second, there is an income-based digital divide between households. Given the average price for data is US $0.68/GB in India, our estimates show that each GB of data costs low-income households (earning less than US$2/day) 3 percent of their monthly income versus 0.2 percent for middle-income households (earning US $10–$20 per day). Finally, intra-household discrimination prevents women from equitably accessing digital devices within the domestic sphere, which in turn widens the gender-based digital divide.[24]

This digital divide is quite stark when viewed in terms of gender and the rural–urban divide; the Internet access statistics are symptomatic of

---

[23] Nikore, "India's Gendered Digital Divide."
[24] Ibid.

a larger problem with access. A National Statistics Office (NSO) report titled "Household Social Consumption on Education" reveals that "4% of the rural population has access to computers as against 23% of the [u]rban population of students above 5 years of age" and that "[i]n rural households, only 10% of students are able to operate computers against 32.4% of students in urban households".[25] With over 68% of India's population living in rural areas, Kullman's claim of a high degree of digital familiarity is incorrect.

THE DIGITAL DIVIDE AND THE PANDEMIC

Such a stark digital divide became all the more obvious during the Covid-19 pandemic. A local English daily reported in an upbeat tone how "some teachers of the humanities stream at Jadavpur University were using the gaming platform, Discord, or digital facilities such as Skype to hold classes from home"[26] after a lockdown was declared; the same daily cited the university's vice-chancellor asking academics "to be 'cautious' about conducting online classes or sharing digital content as many students may not be able to afford a desktop computer or laptop at home, or may be staying in a remote village, with limited or no Internet connectivity".[27] Newspapers also reported that rural students were "climbing trees, hills and trekking through forests to get internet for online classes" highlighting a situation that education policies based on a digital India cannot effectively address.[28] This author's personal experience as the head of another university's English department also bears out the fact from reports of students unable to access classes or afford Internet beyond a specific period or struggling to hand in assignments as they or their relatives did not have smartphones. In the latter cases, they had to write their assignments on paper and take photos that they subsequently sent to the department via someone whose phone they were able to borrow. In an academic interview that this author was part of, multiple students from rural areas appeared for their interviews outdoors on the streets because they could not access the Internet from within their homes. There

---

[25] India Today Web Desk, "Glaring Digital Divide in Education in India."

[26] Chowdhury, "Digital-Divide Caution from Jadavpur VC."

[27] Ibid.

[28] *India Today*, "Rural Students Are Climbing Trees."

are many such stories that are yet to be documented from India, which suffered grievous losses in its population both urban and rural because of a mismanaged lockdown and subsequently, a massive second wave of Covid-19 infections, when vaccination was still not underway.

In the pandemic, especially during the period of the lockdown, all teaching had to be conducted online and even for those who had access to the Internet, power-cuts, inadequate access to Zoom and other such platforms (such as Google Meet and Microsoft Teams mainly but also cheaper options such RingCentral and Jitsi) and the general lack e-learning training proved to be obstacles. In a study on India's digital divide in education during the pandemic conducted by Amanda Glibertson and her team in the University of Melbourne, the following points were raised in addition to what has been mentioned above:

- Many of the low-tech strategies adopted by government and low-fee private schools are remarkably innovative, but they involve far less instructional time than the video lessons of high-fee private schools.
- Ordinarily, more instruction time reduces the gap in learning outcomes between students with parents who have the time, resources and education to support their children's learning—and those who do not.
- Inequalities may also be exacerbated by the expanded role in education that the pandemic has created for EdTech companies in India.
- Many of these services are currently provided for free, but global experience points to tech philanthropy being temporary, and an entry point for future market operations.[29]

If anything, the pandemic served to illustrate the huge digital divide in India's education sector. Shakespeare teaching would also be similarly impacted.

The interviews that the author conducted among university students and teachers who have been teaching Shakespeare during the pandemic provide a mixed picture. Students from Kolkata's Presidency University (formerly Presidency College and Hindoo College where many of the stalwarts of Shakespeare teaching in Bengal have taught) and teaching

---

[29] Gilbertson et al., "India's COVID-19 Divide in Digital Learning."

assistants from New Delhi's Jamia Millia Islamia University were interviewed regarding their experience of Shakespeare pedagogy to get a general idea of what the on-the-ground scenario is. This will be compared with the reportage in local media and the author's personal experience. The consensus among the interviewees was that Google Classroom and Google Meet (both free software or ones that come under the G-Suite license that many Indian universities have obtained) were commonly used. Zahra Rizvi, guest lecturer at Jama Millia Islamia University, New Delhi, in describing her experience of teaching Shakespeare online states:

> Slide and Jamboard whenever required. There is also a Whatsapp group created by the students for discussions and sharing of information outside the classes which take place in [Google] Meet. For sharing visuals, paintings, stage and performance related images, as well as watching specific scenes from adaptations, the "share screen" feature is quite useful. The students use the same feature to present during their group presentations. My students and I also use the Meet chatbox to communicate in case a student's audio isn't working. Additionally, I use online databases and archives.[30]

Her colleague, Jubi John, states

> I would show them clips from the Globe Theatre production of the plays. Google Meet has the feature of sharing the screen so it worked well for my lectures. I feel since drama is performative, hence it was imperative to showcase to my students the range of emotions and the character development of the protagonists. Along with that when I discussed the beginning of Elizabethan theatre, I showed them pictures of the famous theatres of that time, like The Theatre, Rose, The Curtain, The Swan and of course The Globe Theatre. While teaching *The Tempest*, I also made it a point to share with my students how the character Caliban has been represented in art and online archives were the best medium for that. Apart from this, we regularly communicated in the WhatsApp group which again facilitated our interactions.[31]

Together with the G-Suite software, WhatsApp groups are also popular communication groups or discussion boards in India. WhatsApp has been

[30] Rizvi and John, "Teaching Shakespeare in India."

[31] Rizvi and John.

a popular choice for online teaching by default because India has the largest number of WhatsApp users worldwide with 487.5 million far outstripping the next contender Brazil, which has 118.5 million users.[32] With the increasing reach of mobile Internet and WhatsApp versatility in that it enables messaging, audio and video calling as well as sending attachments, the app became a preferred medium of instruction for thousands of teachers caught in the unexpectedness of the pandemic and the sudden demand for online education.

As John argues, it is also important to note the use of multimedia and online archives, here. The key advantages besides the use of multimedia were that students who were reluctant to speak up in physical classes found it easier to communicate via the chatbox. The disadvantages listed were the lack of network access, the need to record lectures and also the lack of peer contact. Students also reiterate similar disadvantages. Sourav Chattopadhyay and Sohini Sengupta, both students of Presidency University Kolkata, complain about frequent network issues and the fact that attending classes in private domestic spaces entails many distractions and that is difficult to focus for two-hour long classes.

Things are not all too grim as far as Shakespeare teaching is concerned as one of them comments that "while the online mode of teaching and the social media-oriented world moves away, somewhat, from the earlier forms of studying and viewing Shakespeare, online focus on Shakespeare can help us view the playwright in many new ways. Digital mapping, archiving, interactive media and viewing of various media representations of Shakespeare's works are among the ways the online format opens itself up for understanding and appreciating Shakespeare in newer ways".[33] Isha Lahiri, another postgraduate student from Presidency University, feels that the online course reduces teacher-student communication and unlike Rizvi and John, for her online courses make students wish to interact even less with their teachers. She is, however, quite familiar with online courses having "been attending online courses on Shakespeare [...] offered by EdX and Coursera in the last 3 years".[34] John and Rizvi both agree that they have used the Folger Shakespeare Library and websites such as Luminarium. Rizvi observes that her "students enjoy sharing

---

[32] Ceci, "Global WhatsApp users in selected countries 2021."

[33] Chattopadhyay and Sengupta, "Teaching Shakespeare in India."

[34] Lahiri, "Teaching Shakespeare in India."

Shakespeare memes and analysing them in class discussions of the texts" while John speaks of a student's "Tumblr post with me about Mercutio's death scene and even a podcast on Spotify".[35] While the shape of Shakespeare teaching is much changed after the pandemic, the earlier lack of performance-based studies of the plays is beginning to be addressed: as Rizvi comments, "I feel Shakespeare particularly requires additional media on the stage, costume, performance, adaptations, etc., and this is the part where teaching Shakespeare online is useful".[36] Judging from the comments of the interviewees, the level of performativity has transcended boundaries between the digital and non-digital and through memes, podcasts and social media that students can create and access easily on smartphones. Even the problems with accessing Shakespeare's language that students repeatedly raised in the interviews are better addressed through online editions. Of course, given the constraints of the pandemic, both Rizvi and John have pointed out that they do not insist on any particular edition in their classes.

In Conclusion: Shakespeare Teaching Reloaded

While there is much promise for the digital medium in Shakespeare teaching the world over, such promise is founded on a key assumption: access. Access can be of multiple kinds, access to the software and hardware, access to the Internet and access to pedagogy. Of course, with the coming of high-speed Internet, the increased number of smartphones, the online courses available on Shakespeare, the global digital archives that make early modern source texts and criticism available and tools such as Zoom and Google Meet that enable online classrooms, Shakespeare teaching is evolving in a new avatar. This image of current digital pedagogy is easily painted; for example, as Richard N. Katz outlines it:

> While it took 1,000 years to raise the tower of higher education, it has taken only 60 years to launch the digital computing and communications revolution. And while the history of computing and communications is faster moving and more boisterous than the history of higher education, it is less subtle and therefore easier to tell. At the most fundamental level,

---

[35] Rizvi and John.

[36] Ibid.

the story of information and communication technology is that of a quest
to put thinking and communicating power everywhere and in everything
and to connect it all.[37]

In this sense, Shakespeare maybe said to have been moved from the ivory
towers of legendary academics to a global cloud, where he is accessible to
everyone. As Laura Estill echoes the question asked by other commenta-
tors: "The prevalence of digital humanities tools in Shakespeare teaching
and research leads Carson and Kirwan to wonder, 'are all Shakespeares
digital now?'".[38] As this article argues, however, the question of *all Shakespeares* is one that is moot—such questions, as well as the tower to cloud
approach, are characteristic of the Global North and assume the absence
of the kind of digital divide that the above sections have pointed to. The
assumption that students today are "digital natives" while instructors are
"digital immigrants"[39] is also one that elides key questions of the digital
divide[40]: students from the Global South certainly do not fall into this
easy categorization of "digital natives".

Following the Digital Humanities scholar, Padmini Ray Murray's
comment, "Your DH is not my DH", Roopika Risam reiterates how
"[e]ngaging with postcolonial digital pedagogy further helps students
understand how print culture has played a role in constructing a world
that privileges the stories, voices, and values of the Global North and
how digital cultures in the twenty-first century reproduce these practices, contributing to the epistemological marginalization of the Global
South".[41] Risam goes on to point at the gaps and silences that remain in
the digital cultural record, which would also pertain to both Shakespeare
scholarship and pedagogy in India. While the digital cultural record is
being made more inclusive by the addition of projects such as *Shakespeare
in Bengal* and MIT Global Shakespeares, there is still much to be done.
Likewise, as the pandemic has cruelly made obvious, the digital divide

---

[37] Katz, *The Tower and the Cloud*, 6.

[38] Estill, "Digital Humanities' Shakespeare Problem."

[39] See Prensky, "Digital Natives, Digital Immigrants?"

[40] Roopika Risam also comments that the term itself "elides and obscures both historical and ongoing oppression towards indigenous communities who are themselves often
relatively disadvantaged in the context of digital divides."

[41] Risam, *New Digital Worlds*, 89.

in Shakespeare pedagogy remains stark as far as access, training and even awareness are concerned.

While the transition of Shakespeare teaching in India from the hallowed legends of a privileged elite, involving teacher and student alike, to a more ecumenical community that can access scholarship on their WhatsApp and Google enabled smartphones is being effected in current times, how far it can reach Indian students both in schools and higher education institutions is something only time will tell; similarly, whether it will encourage rigorous academic scholarship or a more numerous community that shapes its scholarship from dubious sources. For example, in a popular Youtube video, the self-professed National Eligibility Test (NET) expert, Vineet Pandey advises students that if they are asked about the identity of "the dark lady", then they should write "Mary Fitton" and not "Lucy" because the latter was part of the "latest study" (assuming that paper-setters would not know it); he also informs that two of Shakespeare's sonnets were published in a "magazine".[42] Pandey's video has been viewed 76,269 times, outstripping by far the reach that legendary Shakespeare professors of the Hindoo College would have dreamt of. The other end of the spectrum is the extremely scholarly *Shakespeare in Bengal* project that has been mentioned earlier. The Ministry of Human Resource and Development's e-Pathshala program and the Government of India's SWAYAM initiatives also run Shakespeare courses that are better curated. In contrast to the smooth network of global Shakespeare scholarship on an all-pervading cloud that is often imagined in scholarship on digital media emanating from the Global North, the scenario in India is fuzzy and uneven, both in terms of access and scholarliness. As a colonial import that was part of a "civilising mission", Shakespeare Studies has seen many changes in India over the centuries moving from scholarly essays to the multiple-choice question and now to WhatsApp and Google Classroom. Nevertheless, as in the early days of the East India Company, Shakespeare still belongs to an elite, only one that is larger in number—even with greater connectivity and global reach, access remains limited and is a matter of privilege. To end with a modified version of the famous ivory tower to global cloud metaphor, it would be more accurate to view digital Shakespeare in India as still remaining confined to a few ivory towers and

---

[42] Pandey, *Exclusive Lecture On William Shakespeare.*

its cloud-based existence, where it is present at all, is patchy and capricious. The digital, despite its vaunted egalitarianism, merely reinforces the divide that Shakespeare scholarship and pedagogy has always represented, from even before when Macaulay wrote his "Minute" and his praise of Richardson's Shakespeare oratory.

Bibliography

Ashok, Akash Deep. "Do You Know What Shakespeare Wrote about India?" *India Today*, April 23, 2014. https://www.indiatoday.in/world/story/wil lam-shakespeare-wrote-about-india-190124-2014-04-23.

Bhalla, Abhishek, and Ashraf Wani. "'We Need 4G Network': Poor Internet Connectivity Hampers Online Classes, Covid Vaccination Drive in Border Areas of Ladakh—Education Today News." *India Today*, May 25, 2021. https://www.indiatoday.in/education-today/news/story/students-near-lac-ladakh-struggle-with-online-education-due-to-poor-internet-connection-180 6859-2021-05-25.

British Council. "Mix The Play." n.d. Accessed December 20, 2021. https://mixtheplay.britishcouncil.org/.

Ceci, L. "Global WhatsApp Users in Selected Countries 2021." *Statistica*. February 7, 2022. https://www.statista.com/statistics/289778/countries-with-the-most-facebook-users/.

Chakravorty, Swapan Kumar. *Bangalir Engreji Sahitya Charcha*. Kolkata: Anustup, 2011.

Chattopadhyay, Sourav, and Sohini Sengupta. "Teaching Shakespeare in India." 2021. Email.

Chaudhuri, Sukanta. n.d. "Shakespeare in India." *Internet Shakespeare Editions*. https://internetshakespeare.uvic.ca/Library/Criticism/shakespearein/ind ial/.

Chaudhuri, Supriya. "Remembering Shakespeare in India: Colonial and Postcolonial Memory." In *Celebrating Shakespeare: Commemoration and Cultural Memory*, edited by Clara Calvo and Coppélia Kahn, 101–120. Cambridge: Cambridge University Press, 2015. https://doi.org/10.1017/CBO978110 7337466.006.

Chowdhury, Subhankar. "Digital-Divide Caution from Jadavpur VC." *The Telegraph*, April 2, 2020, Web edition. https://www.telegraphindia.com/west-bengal/calcutta/digital-divide-caution-from-jadavpur-vc/cid/1761513.

Dahiya, Hema. "Shakespeare Studies in Colonial Bengal: The Early Phase." PhD Thesis, Sheffield: Sheffield Hallam University, 2011. http://shura.shu.ac.uk/19526/.

"Dhritikanta Lahiri Chowdhury & Sheila Lahiri Chowdhury." *Shakespeare in Bengal* (blog). March 23, 2019. https://shakespeareinbengal.in/dhritikanta-lahiri-chowdhury-sheila-lahiri-chowdhury/.

Estill, Laura. "Digital Humanities' Shakespeare Problem." *Humanities* 8 (1): 45, 2019. https://doi.org/10.3390/h8010045.

Gilbertson, Amanda, Joyeeta Dey, Andrew Deuchar, and Nathan Grills. "India's COVID-19 Divide in Digital Learning." *Pursuit*, August 2021. https://fin danexpert.unimelb.edu.au/news/25243-india%E2%80%99s-covid-19-divide-in-digital-learning.

India Today Web Desk. "Glaring Digital Divide in Education in India: Covid-19 Gives Opportunity for Digital Inclusion." September 11, 2020. https://www.indiatoday.in/education-today/featurephilia/story/glaring-digital-div ide-in-education-in-india-covid-19-digital-inclusion-1720817-2020-09-11.

———. "Rural Students Are Climbing Trees, Hills and Trekking Through Forests to Get Internet for Online Classes." September 24, 2020. https://www.indiatoday.in/education-today/news/story/rural-students-forced-to-climb-trees-and-hills-to-get-internet-for-online-classes-1724976-2020-09-24.

Katz, Richard N. *The Tower and the Cloud: Higher Education in the Age of Cloud Computing*. Washington, DC: Educause, 2010.

Keelery, Sandhya. "India: Internet Penetration Rate 2021." *Statista*. April 27, 2021. https://www.statista.com/statistics/792074/india-internet-penetr ation-rate/.

Kullman, Thomas. "Shakespeare on the Internet: Global and South Asian Appropriations." In *Asian Interventions in Global Shakespeare: 'All the World's His Stage,'* edited by Poonam Trivedi, Paromita Chakravarti, and Ted Motohashi. New York: Routledge, 2020.

Lahiri, Isha. "Teaching Shakespeare in India." 2021. Email.

Macaulay, Thomas Babington. "Minute on Education (1835) by Thomas Babington Macaulay." Project South Asia. October 23, 2016. http://www.columbia.edu/itc/mealac/pritchett/00generallinks/macaulay/txt_minute_education_1835.html.

Nikore, Mitali, and Ishita Uppadhayay. "India's Gendered Digital Divide: How the Absence of Digital Access Is Leaving Women Behind." ORF. August 22, 2021. https://www.orfonline.org/expert-speak/indias-gendered-digital-divide/.

Pandey, Vineet. *Exclusive Lecture on William Shakespeare for NET JRF English Literature by NET Expert Vineet Pandey*. 2019. https://www.youtube.com/watch?v=z5DRM24okwg.

Prensky, Marc. "Digital Natives, Digital Immigrants?" *On the Horizon* 9 (5) 2001. https://www.marcprensky.com/writing/Prensky%20-%20Digital%20N atives,%20Digital%20Immigrants%20-%20Part1.pdf.

Risam, Roopika. *New Digital Worlds: Postcolonial Digital Humanities in Theory, Praxis, and Pedagogy.* Evanston, Illinois: Northwestern University Press, 2018.

Rizvi, Zahra, and Jubi John. "Teaching Shakespeare in India." 2021. Email.

"Shakespeare in Bengal." https://shakespeareinbengal.in/.

Singh, Jyotsna. *Colonial Narratives/Cultural Dialogues: "Discoveries" of India in the Language of Colonialism.* 1st edition. London; New York: Routledge, 1996.

Soofi, Mayank Austen. "Arvind Krishna Mehrotra: Allahabad's Prodigal Poet." *Mint.* November 29, 2014. https://www.livemint.com/Leisure/NBAFvOxrF LQKFtvOeoXvPM/Arvind-Krishna-Mehrotra-Allahabads-prodigal-poet.html.

The Times of India. "5 Plays in Which Shakespeare Mentioned India!" Apr 23, 2020. https://timesofindia.indiatimes.com/life-style/books/features/5-plays-in-which-shakespeare-mentioned-india/photostory/75294427.cms.

Viswanathan, Gauri. *Masks of Conquest: Literary Study and British Rule in India.* Twenty-Fifth Anniversary edition. New York: Columbia University Press, 2014.

Waddell, Karen, and Hedley Sutton. "Shakespeare in India: How Indians Saw and Read the Bard a Hundred Years Back." *Scroll.In.* September 15, 2016. http://scroll.in/article/809215/shakespeare-in-india-an-essay-by-british-raj-era-officer-talks-about-how-we-perceived-the-bard.

Walton, J.K. "Textual Studies." *Shakespeare Survey.* Ed. Kenneth Muir. Cambridge: Cambridge University Press, 1968.

CHAPTER 6

Shakespeare as a Digital Nomad: An Afterword

Alexa Alice Joubin

Abstract The rise of global Shakespeare as an industry and cultural practice—the incorporation of Shakespearean performance in cultural diplomacy and in the cultural marketplace—is aided by digital tools of dissemination and digital forms of artistic expression. Shakespeare has evolved from a cultural nomad in the past centuries—a body of works with no permanent artistic home base—to a digital nomad in the twenty-first century—an artist whose livelihood depends on commissions online and who works from any number of physical locations. The digital sphere is now the most important habitation for global Shakespeare, especially in the era of the pandemic of Covid-19. A nomad may not have a place to call home, but they can also lay claim to any cultural location.

Keywords Nomad · Interface · Digital humanities · Liveness in performance · Covid-19

A. A. Joubin (✉)
Department of English, George Washington University, Washington, DC, USA
e-mail: ajoubin@gwu.edu

© The Author(s), under exclusive license to Springer Nature Switzerland AG 2022
A. Sen (ed.), *Digital Shakespeares from the Global South*,
Global Shakespeares, https://doi.org/10.1007/978-3-031-04787-9_6

In a scene in Armenian-Iranian director Varuzh Karim-Masihi's film *Tardid* (*Doubt*, 2009), an archivist named Siavash is hanging a framed Farsi text, "to be or not to be," on the wall of a dimly lit basement in modern-day Tehran. He proceeds to contemplate the parallels between his life and Hamlet. The Danish prince's speech becomes a tangible artifact in this scene. The framed text on the wall is part of the technologies of representation that are rendering Hamlet's and Siavash's musings in a palpable form of writing. The *mise-en-scène*, with Siavash stating early on that "I've never been very good at making decisions," interfaces Hamlet's soliloquy and Siavash's sensation of being trapped in an interstitial space. In fact, *Hamlet* is more than background noise in *Tardid*; it is a key meta-theatrical device in the film. While investigating the cause of his father's mysterious death, Siavash turns regularly to *Hamlet* for moral guidance. In a particularly rich meta-theatrical moment in the film, Siavash stages a performance of *Hamlet* at the wedding of his mother and uncle to "catch the conscience of the king." Named after the Iranian mythical figure, a symbol of innocence and chastity, the Siyâvash figure, the film's protagonist, carries echoes of both Shakespeare's tragedy, in which Hamlet seeks inner truths, and Ferdowsi's tenth-century Persian epic *Shahnameh* (*The Book of Kings*), in which Siyâvash is compelled to prove his innocence after rejecting advances from his lustful stepmother.

FILMMAKING IN THE GLOBAL SOUTH

This film, little known outside Iran[1] despite its prestigious award,[2] captures several issues raised by the chapters in the present volume, including uneven archival knowledge about and access to the Global South, new ways of interfacing Shakespeare, and Marvin Carlson's theory that performances are always being haunted by technologies of representation and previous iterations of the characters.[3] Old Hamlet's ghost, for instance, appears in a late scene in the film through a mediating mechanism. He communicates with Siavash through a Sufi healer, or an

---

[1] There are only three major peer-reviewed studies of the film: Burnett, *"Hamlet" and World Cinema*, 188–218; O'Brien, "Shakespeare in Iran," *The Palgrave Encyclopedia of Global Shakespeare*, 1–14; and Owlia, "The New Woman and the Oriental Tropes as Portrayed in *Tardid*," 107–118.

[2] Crystal Simorgh award for best film, 27th Fajr International Film Festival, 2009.

[3] Carlson, *The Haunted Stage: The Theatre as Memory Machine*.

intermediary known as *dervish* in southern Iran. While participating in an indigenous Zar spiritual cleansing ritual of dance, Siavash encounters his father's spirit who forcefully inhabits the body of a dancing *dervish*. Interestingly, by the time of this encounter, Siavash is already suspicious of his uncle and has carried out his own investigation. In contrast to Shakespeare's tragedy, the ghost appears quite late in the film and does not give Siavash a revenge mission; his appearance merely completes the puzzle in *Tardid*.

Adaptations do not always have one singular home base. Depending on audiences' film viewing habits and cultural background, they may see, in *Tardid*, traces of life in contemporary Iran, early modern English anxieties about succession, a medieval Danish legend as imagined by Shakespeare, or a combination of all three. *Tardid*'s "minor" style, to use Gilles Deleuze's words, counteracts universalist narrative patterns popularized by Western cinema. By virtue of *Tardid*'s being a Global South film, the characters' "private business is immediately political."[4] A large number of Global South adaptations of Shakespeare, whether aided by digital means of dissemination or not, are constrained in such "minor" spaces of self/representation.

Shakespeare as a Digital Nomad

Thanks to the canonical status of Shakespeare's works, performances of Shakespeare circulate widely, though not always freely, across the globe, giving Shakespeare a global afterlife. However, in what sense is Shakespeare global? Being everything to everyone in every location? Having an equally impactful or accessible presence on every continent? Since *Tardid* does not circulate globally, is it still part of global Shakespeare?

The rise of global Shakespeare as an industry and cultural practice—the incorporation of Shakespearean performance in cultural diplomacy and in the cultural marketplace—is aided by digital tools of dissemination and digital forms of artistic expression. Shakespeare has evolved from a cultural nomad in the past centuries—a body of works with no permanent artistic home base—to a digital nomad in the twenty-first century—an artist whose livelihood depends on commissions online and who works from any number of physical locations. The digital sphere is now the

---

[4] Deleuze, *Cinema 2: The Time-Image*, 220.

most important habitation for global Shakespeare, especially in the era of the pandemic of Covid-19. A nomad may not have a place to call home, but they can also lay claim to any cultural location. *Tardid* is shot in the urban landscape of Tehran with copious references of and allusions to other temporalities and cultural locations, such as life in contemporary Tehran, a tenth-century Persian epic, southern Iranian religious ritual, and early modern English interpretations of a medieval legend.

In her Introduction to this volume, Amrita Sen asks "whose digital Shakespeare is it anyway?" while pointing to the increasingly urgent digital divide across the globe. The standard disclaimer that "your mileage may vary" in terms of experiencing digital performances of Shakespeare does not quite answer these urgent questions about diversity, equity, and inclusion. A digital performance video produced in London but consumed in Tehran, for instance, carries with it culturally specific meanings of these locations. These meanings are filtered and enabled by the screen as interface. Means of access to digital contents also vary greatly between locations due to censorship, uneven valuation of cultural production, and infrastructural inconsistencies.

Contributors to the present volume have more than adequately examined the fraught relations between digital Shakespeare and the Global South. To complement these chapters, in this Afterword, I would like to consider the theoretical ramifications of the idea of Shakespeare as a digital nomad in the era of Covid-19 in the following two areas: the politics of interfacing Shakespeare onscreen and evolving digital archival practices.

The Screening Interface

Shakespearean performance has always been mediated by technologies of representation, both analogue and digital. Screened performance as a narrative medium is governed by the interface between human story-tellers and technologies of representation. Accelerated by the Covid-induced public health measure of social distancing, the past years have witnessed a convergence of what were once distinct media verticals such as film, television, theater, livestream, and other immersive or interactive media forms. Live theater used to be a synchronous communal affair taking place in an architectural space, while performances on private screens were asynchronous, intimate, and individuated. Further, "live" performances used to be distinguished from film—a more editorialized medium—by their cachet of being "ephemeral" and irrecoverable. Now that more and more theatrical and filmic performances are mediated by the same screen interface, these distinctions are going away. Over time, with improvements in communication networks, these changes would redefine the Global South and the Global North.

Just as "the liberation of writing from the book in digital culture" has "changed the ways we make writing perform,"[5] the interface of the screen gives the concept of performance synchronous and asynchronous meanings. The pandemic of COVID-19 has blurred the distinctions between feature films intended for the multiplex and made-for-television, or made-for-streaming, films in terms of funding structures, aspect ratios, and scope of production. These new dynamics extend from multiplex screens to the small screens of laptops, television, tablets, home cinemas, smart phone, and other personalized interfaces.

The interfaces and the channels of distribution are merging quickly. Netflix, a purveyor of streaming products, is now a global producer of original contents in the forms of both films and television series. These products are intended for streaming rather than collective consumption in multiplexes. Amazon, having acquired the Metro-Goldwyn-Mayer movie company in 2021, is also capitalizing on its Prime Video streaming platform. Amazon Studios have already (co)produced a hundred original films, including Richard Eyre's 2018 *King Lear*, starring Anthony Hopkins in the lead role and streamed as part of Amazon Prime.

In the golden era of Shakespeare on television (1944–1971), most TV versions were based on successful stage performances. In contrast, in our times, there is no longer a hierarchical order of page-to-stage-to-television-to-film. This is due to the lockdown as a public health measure during the pandemic and due to the prevalence of streaming technologies already in place before 2020. Before the pandemic, more and more stage productions had been broadcast live, or in recorded formats, such as the Royal Shakespeare Theatre's RSC-Live series, to audiences in theaters. Now, an even larger number of born-digital, or re-mastered, performances reached audiences directly on the small screen. It is no longer as meaningful to distinguish between "live" productions, multiplex films, and made-for-small-screen films.

It is now commonplace to integrate Shakespeare in traditional film formats on the big screen into personalized experiences on the small

---

[5] Worthen, "Posthuman Shakespeare performance studies," 215–222; 217.

screen for personal entertainment or for education. Competing digital interfaces, as Thomas Cartelli observes, "reduce the objective of feature film presentation in fixed screening spaces to one among many reception/display options."[6] One challenge for the study of digital Shakespeare now is that the interface often makes itself transparent even though it is generating the dramaturgical meanings central to the narratives. The screen interface immerses audiences in an alternate universe in such a way that audiences rarely question the screen's aesthetic function.

COVID-19 accelerated the global processes of interfacing Shakespeare onscreen. Theater director Erin B. Mee writes optimistically that the pandemic has created "an exciting new performance environment," bringing artists and audiences together "from numerous nations" and creating "new possibilities for collaboration." Digital forms of video communication have enabled "artists from around the world" to gather in virtual spaces "playing to international audiences rather than ... to people who can get to a particular piece of real estate" in time.[7]

The global pandemic has further expanded the idea of liveness. The new genre of born-digital performances has redefined the notion of liveness as merely "a temporal and spatial entity."[8] Attending a live event no longer entails being physically in the same space at the same time, breathing the same air (and, after 2020, thereby sharing the same virus). Liveness has evolved to become a synchronous concept. As Philip Auslander critiqued in 2008, more than a decade before the pandemic-fueled rise of performances on such video conferencing platforms as Zoom, the now antiquated idea of liveness reduces "live performance and its present mediatized environment" to a "binary opposition of the live and the mediatized" in which the live event is "real" and that mediatized events are "secondary and somehow artificial reproductions of the real."[9]

As the ideological structures governing liveness and artistic prestige change, so do the possibilities of art making. Asynchronous digital videos in the form of archival streams do not so much replicate

---

[6] Cartelli, *Reenacting Shakespeare in the Shakespeare Aftermath: The Intermedial Turn and Turn to Embodiment*, 48.

[7] Mee and TDR Editors, "Forum: After COVID-19, What?" 191–224; 208–209.

[8] Sullivan, "The Audience is Present: Aliveness, Social Media and the Theatre Broadcast Experience," 59–75.

[9] Auslander, *Liveness: Performance in a Mediatized Culture*, 3.

theatrical experiences as they enable experiential and affective immersiveness on personal electronic devices for private consumption. Blurring the boundary between film and theater, both genres are detached from the palpable bodily presence of actors. Notably, viewers' own subjectivity becomes disembodied just as that of the actors, but in the process they build a community through "virtual co-presence."[10]

Three observations can be made about these instances of interfacing Shakespeare onscreen. First, the screen as interface has created deep structural connections among even works that seem to be isolated instances of artistic creation. The connections extend through the cultural practice of interfacing different media, such as film, theater, and visual arts. The cases above relate more frequently to one another, through the screening interface, than to Shakespeare as sanctified source material.

Secondly, more and more works are products of meta-cinematic and meta-theatrical operations. The meanings of adaptations such as *Tardid* are shaped by their uses of Shakespearean motifs and quotes (such as "to be or not to be") as interface. The archetype of Hamlet is deployed to capture the figure of the despondent in distinctively local contexts.

Thirdly, the interface culture has given rise to digitally enhanced global Shakespeare performances. The "to be or not to be" speech is familiar enough to serve as an interface between a character's suffering and an index of intelligence, such as Siavash in *Tardid*. The pandemic has highlighted the importance of networks of instantaneous cross references as well as localized, embodied knowledge about Shakespeare. The interface-driven screen culture has de-centered Shakespeare's singularity—the perceived infinite value of the canon—by turning Shakespearean artifacts into a heterotopia. In time, this interface may deconstruct the division between the Global North and the Global South.

ARCHIVAL SILENCE

At stake in global artistic exchanges are not only politics of access and visibility but also variegated, distributed, and user data-driven archives that act as gatekeepers and artistic agents. It is through archives that stage and screen performances of Shakespeare become "teachable" moments and

[10] Aebischer, *Viral Shakespeare Performance in the Time of Pandemic*, 11.

subjects for scholarly research. Over the past decade, digital artifacts— digital performance videos, user-generated tag clouds and comments, Twitter feeds—have become multimodal, common objects of study for researchers, educators, and students, changing scholarly communication practices in disseminating research findings and the praxis of humanistic inquiry.[11] This development has profound implications for the study of arts in the Global South in terms of the uneven power structure and access issues, though we may only see the results in the next decade.

There are, of course, caveats beyond digital ephemerality. As much as archives may preserve traces of the past, they are also "sites of loss, effacement and forgetting, where some voices are silent and silenced."[12] Open-access digital archives of performances may democratize access and even enhance content creation, but they may not be able to feature voices from the Global North and the Global South in equal measures in playable media.

Take, for instance, the *MIT Global Shakespeares* (https://globalshakes peares.mit.edu/) that I co-founded with Peter S. Donaldson. Aiming to provide vetted, crowd-sourced performance videos that are open-access with permalinks, the open-access digital performance video archive offers free online access to performances from many parts of the world as well as peer-reviewed essays and vetted metadata provided by scholars and educators in the field. Deeply collaborative in nature with 9 regional editors and 4 affiliated projects, the MIT platform publishes vetted video, metadata, and peer-reviewed analyses of performances. The project has spotlighted artistic and academic works by people of color, created undergraduate and doctoral internships and research positions in digital publishing, and enabled students, artists, and researchers to access primary research materials freely.

Despite our effort, there are gaps. In terms of South American representation, we have curated a large number of Brazilian productions, with Argentinian works coming in second. The coverage map of sub-Saharan African continent is largely blank, except for co-productions or works that have toured to South Africa, such as Antony Sher and John Kani's *King*

[11] Joubin, "Global Shakespeare 2.0 and the Task of the Performance Archive," 38–51.

[12] Hodder, "On Absence and Abundance: Biography as Method in Archival Research," 452–439; 452.

Lear-inspired two-people show, *Kunene and the King* (Royal Shakespeare Company and Cape Town's Fugard Theatre, 2019).

If global Shakespeare seems to be all over the map or missing from some maps altogether, it is because, first, many productions do not have a single point of cultural origin, and second, our collective knowledge about the Global South is contingent upon cultural and political forces. There is archival silence that results from censorship as well as scholars' over reliance on polity-driven historiography—narratives about art that focus on national political histories rather than cultural exchange beyond the borders of nation-states. Maps are often used as markers of geopolitical power, which is why we have detailed histories of national Shakespeares in the Anglophone world and more traditional postcolonial contexts, but relevantly few accounts of non-mainstream works from the Global South, such as *Tardid*.

Mental maps of the world that are informed by area studies models inadvertently create unknowable objects by flattening the artworks against national profiles. As visually appealing as the map is as a navigational and heuristic tool, its clean lines between nations obscure the fact that many productions do not have one single home. As such, such a map does not seem to promote an appreciation of transnational cultural flows or the fact that while Lotfi Achour's *Macbeth: Leila and Ben, a Bloody History* hailed from Tunisia, the Franco-Arabic company APA's production—with a French translation of Heiner Müller's German translation—resisted a unified identity. It incorporated traditions of the European experimental theater, the Arab Middle East, and Africa.

Attempts to map the itineraries of global Shakespeare reveal that there is a limit to Shakespeare's global reach. The gaps are inevitable when archives are themselves highly selective repository of memories. Further, sensitive or subversive texts can be removed from sight, leading to silenced or redacted stories. The stories an archive tells may be curated, censored, and distorted by native informants and global producers, or otherwise filtered by financial circumstances or ideological preferences. However, what is not there is as important as the canonical performances.

Most archives have not caught up to the fact that Shakespeare is now a digital nomad. There are two implications of silences in the archive. First, silences or gaps in a body of records may reflect certain realities in the world the archive is trying to map. There seem to be no significant Shakespeare traditions in the Antarctic, Iceland, Greenland, Fiji, Tristan da Cunha, Mongolia, Iran, and in large swaths of Sub-Saharan Africa except for South Africa. Materials from these areas are therefore sparse or missing in the archive. These gaps may well reflect an actual dearth of Shakespearean performances in those places, but the gaps may also be a result of scholars' limited linguistic repertoire or cross-cultural interest.

Second, authorities may deny scholar-archivists full access to sensitive or censored archives for any number of reasons. Censorship not only impedes access to archives but also compromises academic freedom. For example, even when scholars are able to locate politically sensitive materials pertaining to performances of *Hamlet* in post-Arab Spring Egypt, they may not be able to discuss them in public because of concerns for the safety of their collaborators and interviewees who are still living in those countries. They may not be able to publish their findings because they are concerned that they will be banned from entering those countries on future research trips or will not receive funding from those governments.

Archival silence occurs due to censorship and sometimes lack of artists' consent. The gap in our archival knowledge is also caused by Covid-induced, citizenship-based international travel bans or restrictions that hinder mobility and access.[13] The full ramification of Covid-19 on the humanistic inquiry will only be known in the decades to come.

In our study of the Global South, the archival silence constitutes productive negative evidence in the archaeological and anthropological senses. Archival silence compels us to rethink our criteria and frames of reference. On one hand, while postcolonial critics commonly privilege Global South works that critique the role of Western hegemony, the meanings of Shakespeare in such places as South Africa, Brazil, and India are not always determined by colonial frames of reference. On the other hand, as chapters in our book capably show, the absence of a coherent, constructed Shakespeare tradition in certain place does not mean there are no local engagements with Shakespearean material.

It is my hope that, in the not-so-distant future, those of us at the presumptive center of the Shakespeare industry will be hanging on our

---

[13] Since blanket travel bans are "not effective in suppressing international spread," the WHO has called on governments to stop the practice which "may discourage transparent and rapid reporting of emerging" viral variant of concern. WHO, "Statement on the tenth meeting of the International Health Regulations (2005) Emergency Committee regarding the coronavirus disease (COVID-19) pandemic," *WHO News*, January 19, 2022, https://www.who.int/news/item/19-01-2022-statement-on-the-tenth-meeting-of-the-international-health-regulations-(2005)-emergency-committee-regarding-the-corona virus-disease-(covid-19)-pandemic.

proverbial walls a framed speech by characters such as Siavash, rather than witnessing more Siavashs carrying on Shakespeare's "dying voice" (*Hamlet* 5.2.308) only to be silenced by the archives.[14]

REFERENCES

Aebischer, Pascale, *Viral Shakespeare Performance in the Time of Pandemic.* Cambridge: Cambridge University Press, 2021.

Auslander, Philip, *Liveness: Performance in a Mediatized Culture*, 2nd edition. New York: Routledge, 2008.

Burnett, Mark Thornton, *"Hamlet" and World Cinema.* Cambridge: Cambridge University Press, 2019.

Carlson, Marvin, *The Haunted Stage: The Theatre as Memory Machine.* Ann Arbor: University of Michigan Press, 2003.

Cartelli, Thomas, *Reenacting Shakespeare in the Shakespeare Aftermath: The Intermedial Turn and Turn to Embodiment.* New York: Palgrave, 2019.

Deleuze, Gilles, *Cinema 2: The Time-Image*, trans. Hugh Tomlinson and Robert Galeta. Minneapolis: University of Minnesota Press, 1989.

Hodder, Jake. "On Absence and Abundance: Biography as Method in Archival Research," *Area* 49.4 (2017): 452–439; 452.

Joubin, Alexa Alice, "Global Shakespeare 2.0 and the Task of the Performance Archive," *Shakespeare Survey* 64 (2011): 38–51. https://ajoubin.org/.

Mee, Erin B., and TDR Editors, "Forum: After COVID-19, What?" *TDR: The Drama Review* 64.3 (Fall, 2020): 191–224; 208–209.

O'Brien, Shauna, "Shakespeare in Iran," *The Palgrave Encyclopedia of Global Shakespeare*, ed. Alexa Alice Joubin, Ema Vyroubalova, and Elizabeth Pentland. New York: Palgrave Macmillan, 2021), 1–14. https://doi.org/10. 1007/978-3-319-99378-2_23-1.

Owlia, Shekufeh, "The New Woman and the Oriental Tropes as Portrayed in *Tardid*," *Culture-blind Shakespeare: Multiculturalism and Diversity*, ed. Maryam Beyad and Ali Salami. Newcastle-upon-Tyne: Cambridge Scholars Publishing, 2016, 107–118.

Shakespeare, William, *The Oxford Shakespeare: The Complete Works*, 2nd edition, ed. John Jowett, William Montgomery, Gary Taylor, and Stanley Wells. Oxford: Oxford University Press, 2005.

---

[14] William Shakespeare, *The Oxford Shakespeare: The Complete Works*, 2nd edition, ed. John Jowett, William Montgomery, Gary Taylor, and Stanley Wells (Oxford: Oxford University Press, 2005), 716.

Sullivan, Erin, "The Audience is Present: Aliveness, Social Media and the Theatre Broadcast Experience," *Shakespeare and the 'Live' Theatre Broadcast Experience*, ed. Pascale Aebischer, Susanne Greenhalgh and Laurie E. Osbourne. London: Bloomsbury, 2018, 59–75.

Worthen, W.B., "Posthuman Shakespeare Performance Studies," *Postmedieval: A Journal of Medieval Cultural Studies* 1.1–2 (2010): 215–222.

INDEX